First World War
and Army of Occupation
War Diary
France, Belgium and Germany

4 DIVISION
10 Infantry Brigade
Princess Louise's (Argyll & Sutherland Highlanders)
1/7th Battalion
1 December 1914 - 30 June 1915

WO95/1481/2

The Naval & Military Press Ltd
www.nmarchive.com
Published in association with The National Archives

Published by

The Naval & Military Press Ltd

Unit 10 Ridgewood Industrial Park,

Uckfield, East Sussex,

TN22 5QE England

Tel: +44 (0) 1825 749494

www.naval-military-press.com

www.nmarchive.com

This diary has been reprinted in facsimile from the original. Any imperfections are inevitably reproduced and the quality may fall short of modern type and cartographic standards.

© **Crown Copyright**
Images reproduced by permission of The National Archives, London, England, 2015.

Contents

Document type	Place/Title	Date From	Date To
Heading	4 Division ID Inf Bde 7 Bn Argyll & Sutherland HDRS 1914 Dec-1916 Feb		
Heading	4th Division 10th Bde 1/7th Battn Argyle & Sutherland Highlanders January & February 1916 From to 154 Bde 51st Div, 1st March 1916		
Heading	10th Brigade 4th Division 1/7th Battalion Argyle & Sutherland Highlanders January 1916		
War Diary		01/01/1916	31/01/1916
Heading	10th Brigade 4th Division Battalion Transferred To 154th Bde; 51st Division 1st March 1916 1/7th Battalion Argyle & Sutherland Highlanders February 1916		
War Diary		01/02/1916	29/02/1916
Heading	4th Division 10th Infantry Bde 7th Battalion Argyle & Sutherland Highlanders July To December 1915		
Heading	10th Inf. Bde. 4th Div. 7th Battn. The Argyle & Sutherland Highlanders July 1915		
War Diary		01/07/1915	31/07/1915
Miscellaneous	Casualty Lists		
Miscellaneous	1/9th Bn, Argyll & Suthd. Higherlanders	01/07/1915	01/07/1915
Miscellaneous	1/9th Bn, Argyll & Suthd. Higherlanders	02/07/1915	02/07/1915
Miscellaneous	1/9th Bn, Argyll & Suthd. Higherlanders	04/07/1915	04/07/1915
Miscellaneous	1/9th Bn, Argyll & Suthd. Highrs	07/07/1915	07/07/1915
Miscellaneous	1/9th Bn. Argyll & Suthd. Highlanders	07/07/1915	07/07/1915
Miscellaneous	1/9th Bn. Argyll & Sutherland. Higherlanders	08/07/1915	08/07/1915
Miscellaneous	1/9th Bn. Argyll & Sutherland Highrs	09/07/1915	09/07/1915
Miscellaneous	1/9th Bn. Argyll & Suthd. Highrs	10/07/1915	10/07/1915
Miscellaneous	1/9th Bn. Argyll & Suthd. Highers.	11/07/1915	11/07/1915
Miscellaneous	1/9th Bn. Argyll & Suthd. Highers.	12/07/1915	12/07/1915
Miscellaneous	1/9th Bn. Argyll & Sutherland Highlanders	12/07/1915	12/07/1915
Miscellaneous	1/9th Bn. Argyll & Suthd Higherlanders	14/07/1915	14/07/1915
Miscellaneous	1/9th Bn. Arg & Suthd. Highers.	15/07/1915	15/07/1915
Miscellaneous	1/9th Bn, Argyll & Suthd. Highlanders.	16/07/1915	16/07/1915
Miscellaneous	1/9th Bn. Argyll & Suthd. Highrs.	17/07/1915	17/07/1915
Miscellaneous	1/9th Bn. Argyll & Suthd Highrs.	18/07/1915	18/07/1915
Miscellaneous	1/9th Bn. Argyll & Suthd. Highrs.	13/07/1915	13/07/1915
Miscellaneous	1/9th Bn. Argyll & Suthd. Highrs.	18/07/1915	18/07/1915
Heading	10th Inf. Bde. 4th Div. 7th Battn. The Argyll & Sutherland Highlanders August 1915		
War Diary		01/08/1915	31/08/1915
Heading	10th Inf. Bde. 4th Div. 7th Battn The Argyll & Sutherland Highlanders September 1915		
War Diary		01/09/1915	30/09/1915
Heading	10th Inf. Bde. 4th Div. 7th Battn. The Argyll & Sutherland Highlanders October 1915		
War Diary		01/10/1915	31/10/1915
Heading	10th Inf. Bde. 4th Div. 7th Battn. Argyll & Sutherland Highlander November 1915		
War Diary		01/11/1915	30/11/1915

Heading	10th Inf. Bde. 4th Div 7th Battn. The Argyll & Sutherland Highlanders December 1915		
War Diary		01/12/1915	31/12/1915
Heading	4th Division 10th Infantry Bde 7th To 9th Battn Argyll & Sutherland Highlanders 1914 Dec-1915 Jan		
Heading	Army Troops 7th Argyll & Sutherland H.Q. Vol I 1-31.12.14		
War Diary		01/12/1914	31/12/1914
Heading	10th Inf. Bde. 4th Div 7th Battn. The Argyll & Sutherland Highlanders January 1915		
War Diary		01/01/1915	31/01/1915
Heading	10th Inf. Bde. 4th Div. 7th Battn. The Argyll & Sutherland Highlanders February 1915		
War Diary	Armentieres	01/02/1915	28/02/1915
Heading	10th Inf. Bde, 4th Div 7th Battn. The Argyll & Sutherland Highlanders March 1915		
War Diary	La Grande Manque	01/03/1915	30/03/1915
Heading	10th Inf. Bde. 4th Div. 7th Battn. The Argyll & Sutherland Highlanders April 1915		
War Diary		01/04/1915	30/04/1915
Heading	10th Inf Bde. 4th Div. 7th Battn. The Argyll & Sutherland Highlanders May 1915		
War Diary		01/05/1915	31/05/1915
Heading	Account of Action 24th May		
Miscellaneous	The Historical Section (Military Branch)	11/08/1925	11/08/1925
Miscellaneous	Major W. McCracken's Account		
Miscellaneous	Lieut-Colonel J.M Scott's Account	24/05/1915	24/05/1915
Miscellaneous	Pencil Note On Back Of Old Envelope	04/06/1915	04/06/1915
Miscellaneous	O.C. Depot. Argyle And Sutherland Highlanders	25/05/1915	25/05/1915
Miscellaneous	4th Division G.L. 896 24th		
Miscellaneous	To 28th Division B.M.181		
Miscellaneous	O.C. Administrative Centre		
Miscellaneous	2/7th Arg. and Suth'd Hrs Orderly Room	07/06/1915	07/06/1915
Heading	Casualty Lists		
Miscellaneous	1/9th Battn Argyll & Suthd: Hrs.	04/05/1915	04/05/1915
Miscellaneous	1/9th Battn Argyll & Suthd: Hrs.	11/05/1915	11/05/1915
Miscellaneous	1/9th Battn Argyll & Suthd: Hrs.	12/05/1915	12/05/1915
Miscellaneous	1/9th Bn. The Argyll & Sutherland Highlanders	16/05/1915	16/05/1915
Miscellaneous	1/9th Bn The Argyll & Sutherland Higherlanders	18/05/1915	18/05/1915
Miscellaneous	1/9th Argyll & Sutherland Highlanders	20/05/1915	20/05/1915
Miscellaneous	1/9th Bn, Argyll & Sutherland Highlanders	21/05/1915	21/05/1915
Miscellaneous	1/9th Bn.The Argyll & Sutherland Highlanders	21/05/1915	21/05/1915
Miscellaneous	9th Argyle & Sutherland Highlanders		
Miscellaneous	1/9th Bn, Argyll & Sutherland Highlanders T.F.		
Miscellaneous	1/9th Bn. Argyll & Sutherland Highrs.	25/05/1915	25/05/1915
Miscellaneous	1/9th Bn, Argyll & Sutherland Highdrs	31/05/1915	31/05/1915
Heading	10th Inf. Bde. 4th Div 7th & 9th Battns. The Argyll & Sutherland Highlanders (Composite Battalion) June 1915		
War Diary		01/06/1915	30/06/1915
Heading	Casualty Lists		
Miscellaneous	1/9th Batt. Argylle & Sutherland Highlanders	01/06/1915	01/06/1915
Miscellaneous	1/9th Battn Argyll & Sutherland Hdrs	02/06/1915	02/06/1915
Miscellaneous	1/9th Argyll & Sutherland Hdrs		
Miscellaneous	1/9th Batt. Argyll & Sutherland Hdrs	06/06/1915	06/06/1915
Miscellaneous	1/9th Bn. Argyll And Sutherland Highlanders	10/06/1915	10/06/1915

Miscellaneous	1/9th Bn. Argyll & Sutherland Highrs	17/06/1915	17/06/1915
Miscellaneous	1/9th Bn. Argyll & Sutherland Highlanders	23/06/1915	23/06/1915
Miscellaneous	1/9th Bn. Argyll & Suther. Highlanders	27/06/1915	27/06/1915
Miscellaneous	1/9th Bn. Argyll & Sutherland Highlanders	28/06/1915	28/06/1915
Miscellaneous	1/9th Bn. Argyll & Sutherland Highlanders	30/06/1915	30/06/1915

4 DIVISION

10 INF BDE

7 BN ARGYLL & SUTHERLAND HDRS

1914 DEC — 1916 FEB

ABSORBED 9 BN 1915 MAY

TO 51 DIV 154 BDE

9 BN RESUMED AS INDEPENDENT FORMATION ON 4.7.15 AND TRANSFERRED TO 6 CORPS TROOPS

4th Division
10th Bde
1/7th Battn
Argyle & Sutherland Highlanders

January & February 1916
Trans to 154 Bde, 51st Div,
1st March 1916

FROM

10th Brigade.

4th Division.

1/7th BATTALION

ARGYLE & SUTHERLAND HIGHLANDERS

JANUARY A 1 9 1 6

Army Form C. 2118.

7th ARGYLL & SUTHERLAND HIGHDRS

WAR DIARY
or
INTELLIGENCE SUMMARY

(Erase heading not required.)   Ref MAP - FRANCE - 57 D.

1916 Hour, Date, Place	Summary of Events and Information	Remarks and references to Appendices
January 1.	In Billets - 10th Bde reserve - at BEAUSSART	
2/9.	Provided working parties for R.E. on 1st and 2nd line Trenches	
10	In billets	
11/16	Provided working parties	
17	In billets	
18/24	Provided working parties	
25	In billets	
26/31	Provided working parties	
27	2 Officers (Lieut S. Cunningham and 2nd Lt J.C. McCracken) and 1. O.R. reinforcements arrived.	

W.J. Duff Lt. Col.
Comdg 7th Bn A & S Highlanders

10th Brigade.

4th Division.

Battalion transferred to 154th Bde; 51st Division

1st March 1916.

1/7th BATTALION

ARGYLE & SUTHERLAND HIGHLANDERS

FEBRUARY 1 9 1 6

1/7th Argyll & Sutherland Highlanders

Army Form C. 2118.

WAR DIARY
or
INTELLIGENCE SUMMARY

(Erase heading not required.)

Ref Map - France 57 D

Hour, Date, Place	Summary of Events and Information	Remarks and references to Appendices
February 1	At BEAUSSART in 10th Bde Reserve. Provided working parties for R.E. 2/Lt G. Fraser arrived as reinforcement.	
2	Provided working parties.	
3	In billets. Capt. J. Murdoch RAMC. relieved Lt. D.S. Campbell as Medical Officer	
4	Moved into rest billets at MONDICOURT. (Transport at GRENAS)	
5	In billets cleaning clothing and equipment	
6	Route marches by Companies	
7/8	Physical training and elementary squad drill.	
8	2/Lt W.S. Lawson arrived as reinforcement.	
9	Battn route march in forenoon, in afternoon 1 Coy digging trenches; 1 Coy at Musketry	
10	Training.	

4th Division

10th Infantry Bde.

7th Battn. Argyll Sutherland
                  Highlanders

July to December
    1915

10th Inf.Bde.
4th Div.

7th BATTN. THE ARGYLL & SUTHERLAND HIGHLANDERS.

J U L Y

1 9 1 5

(Note: The 7th & 9th Battns. The
Argyll & Sutherland High-
landers were organised as
a Composite Battalion on
27.5.15. Independent
formations were resumed
on 21.7.15, the 9th Battn.
being transferred to VI.
Corps as Corps Troops).

Attached:

Casualty Lists.

Army Form C. 2118.

1st to 20th July — Composite Battⁿ A. & S. Highlanders
20th to 31st July — 7th Battⁿ A. & S. H.

WAR DIARY
~~INTELLIGENCE SUMMARY~~
(Erase heading not required.)

Ref. Map Sheet 28. (Ypres)

Instructions regarding War Diaries and Intelligence Summaries are contained in F. S. Regs., Part II. and the Staff Manual respectively. Title pages will be prepared in manuscript.

Hour, Date, Place	Summary of Events and Information	Remarks and References to Appendices
1915 July 1st to 7th.	Composite Battⁿ at S.H. in Dug-outs at B.27. Provided carrying and working parties for R.E. and battalions in firing line.	
July 8th — 8 p.m. July 9th to 20th. July 20th.	Composite Battⁿ proceeded to Rest Billets at HOFLAND – HOUTEKERQUE. In Billets. Separation of 7th and 9th Argylls carried out in accordance with 2nd Army telegram of this date.	
July 21st. July 22nd — 2 p.m. July 23rd — 4 A.M.	7. at S.H. in billets. Battⁿ proceeded to GODEWAERSVELDE Entrained for DOULLENS, where the battⁿ detrained at 2 p.m. and marched to VAUCHELLES.	
July 24/25/26 July 27 — 6 p.m. July 28 to 31st.	In Billets at VAUCHELLES. Battⁿ proceeded to billets at BEAUSSART. Provided working parties for R.E. and battⁿ is firing line and continued company training	

M.K. Batt Capt.
O.C. 7th A. & S. H.

CASUALTY LISTS.

CASUALTIES.   No 1 District.

1/9th Bn. Argyll & Suthd. Highlanders

Regtl. No.	Rank & Name.	Casualty.	By Whom Repd.	P.R.
2545.	Pte. Gray G.	Transferred to England 4-6-15.	O.C. Hosp Ship ST David 5-6-15.	W.
2985.	L/Cpl. Fraser J.	Wounded & Missing. (Suspicious Case.)	O.C. Battn. 28-6-15.	W.

1-7-15.   J A Hood. Cpl.

CASUALTIES. No.1 District.

1/9th Bn. Argyll & Sutherland Highlanders.

Regtl. No.	Rank & Name.	Casualty.	By Whom Reported.	P.R.
2292.	Pte. Ferrie. D.	Killed in Action.	O.C.Battn. 30-6-15.	N.

2-7-15.   J.A.Hood. Cpl.

CASUALTIES No.1 District.

1/9th Bn. Argyll & Sutherland Higherlanders

Regtl. No.	Rank & Name	Casualty.	By Whom Reported.	P.R.
2549	Pte. Hughes P.	Transferred to England. (Unfit for Duty.) 30-6-15-	O.C 2 Terr. Base Depot.	S.
2412.	Pte. Todd D.	ditto.	ditto.	W.
2550.	Pte Hoskins G.	To Duty. 1-7-15.	O.C. Con Depot.	W.

4-7-15.

J.X.Hood. Cpl.

CASUALTIES.   No 1 District.

1/9th Bn. Argyll & Suthd. Highrs.

Regtl. No.	Rank & Name.	Casualty.	By Whom Reported.	P.R.
1413	Sgt. McLachlan W.	Transferred to England 29-4-15.	O.C. 5 Gen. Hospital.	W.
2065.	Pte. Thomson M.	To Duty. 3-7-15-	O.C 2 Terr. Base Depot.	W.
2027.	Pte. Lees W.	ditto.	ditto.	S.

7-7-15-

J A Hood. Cpl.

CASUALTIES   No.1.DISTRICT

1/9th.Bn.ARGYLL & SUTHERLAND HIGHLANDERS.

Regtl. No.	Rank and Name	Casualty	By whom reported	BY whom reported.	Prevs. reptd.
3199.	Pte. Anderson T.	G.S.W.SHOULDER & LEFT KNEE - Admitted 10 Casualty Clearing Station 9/5/15. DIED OF WOUNDS.10/5/15.		O.C.10 Cas.Clg. Station. 4/7/15.	W'dd.
2994.	Pte. Stirling, W.	Wounded in Action 1/7/15.		O.C.Bn. 3/7/15.	Nil.

7/7/15.

J A Hood
Cpl
9th A S Hrs

CASUALTIES.   No.1 District,

1/9th Bn Argyll & Sutherland Higherlanders.

Regtl No.	Rank & Name.	Casualty.	By Whom Reported.	P.R.
2075	Pte. Barlas W.	Wounded in Action 2-7-15	O.C. Bn. 3-7-15,	Not by O.C.Bn.

8-7-15.

JA Hood.
Capt.

Lowe
1/7

CASUALTIES.   No 2 District.

1/9th Bn. Argyll & Sutherland Highrs.

Regtl. No.	Rank & Name.	Casualty.	By Whom Reported.	P.R.
2643.	Pte. Robertson R.C.	Killed in Action 5-4-15.	O.C.Battn. 10-4-15.	R.

9-7-15.

CASUALTIES. No. 1 District.

1/9th Bn. Argyll & Suthd Highrs.

Regtl. No.	Rank & Name.	Casualty.	By Whom Reported.	P.R.
2715.	Pte. Jamieson R.	Transferred to England 5-5-15.	O.C.16 Gen. Hospital.	S.
2177.	Pte. Wildon R.	Transferred to England	O.C.T.F.Records. 6-7-15.	W.
1717.	Pte. Sheridan J.	To Duty.	O.C.2 Terr Base Depot 8-7-15.	W

10-7-15.

CASUALTIES.   No.1 District.

                    1/9
                    1/9th Bn. Argyll & Suthd. Highrs.

Regtl, No.	Rank & Name.	Casualty.	By Whom Reported.	P.R.
936	Sgt. Duncan G.	Died of Wounds 28-5-15.	O.C. 3 Cas. Clearing Station 8-7-15.	W.
1840	Sgt. Ronald W.	Transferred to England. Marked P.B.	O.C. 2 Terr Base 8-7-15.	S.
1425	Drm. Cairns J.	Ditto.	Ditto.	W.

11-7-15.

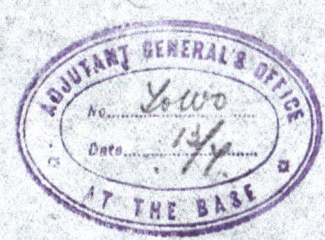

CASUALTIES. No.1 District.

1/9th Bn. Argyll & Suthd Highrs.

Regtl. No.	Rank & Name.	Casualty.	By Whom Reported.	P.R.
1732.	Pte. Sneddon A.	To England	O.C.T.F.Records. 22-6-15.	N.
2645.	L/Cpl. Robertson J.	Killed in Action. 10-5-15.	O.C.Battn. 7-7-15.	N.

12-7-15.

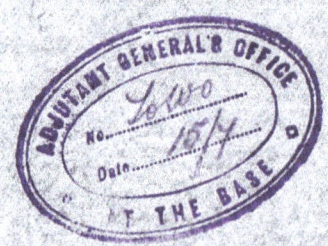

CASUALTIES   No. 9. DISTRICT

1/9th. Bn. ARGYLL & SUTHERLAND HIGHLANDERS.

Regtl. No.	Rank and Name	CASUALTY	By whom reptd.	Prevs reptd
2345.	Sgt. Jarrett T.H.	When in England on Leave, reported by O.C. 131st. Field Ambulance to be suffering from Piles. - Transferred to 2/9th.Bn. Argyll & Suth. Highlrs, England 9/7/15.	Reported by Officer i/c Terr. Force Records, Perth. 10/7/15.	Nil.

12/7/15.

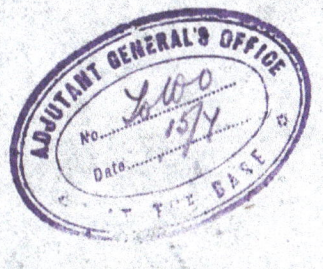

CASUALTIES.   No. 1 District

1/9th Bn. Argyll & Suthd Higherlanders.

Regtl.No.	Rank & Name.	Casualty.	By, Whom Reported.	P.R.
LIEUT.	OWEN A.O.	PRISONER OF WAR.	Reported O.C. Missing. Battn. 9-7-15.	
1593.	Pte. Crearer J.	Believed to be Prisoner of War.	Do.	do.

14-7-15.

CASUALTIES.	No.1 District.

1/9th Bn. Arg & Suthd Highrs.

Regtl. No.	Rank & Name.	Casualty.	By Whom Reported.	P.R.
2624.	Pte. McGrate A.	Transferred to England. 4-6-15.	O.C. Base Commandant 28-6-15.	S.

1-7-15.

J A Hood Cpl

CASUALTIES.   No 1 District.

1/9th Bn. Argyll & Suthd Highlanders.

Regtl No.	Rank & Name	Casualty	By Whom Reported.	P.R.
2517.	Pte. Cowden J.	Wounded & Missing (Suspicious Case.)	OC Battn 7-7-15.	Wounded

16-7-15.

CASUALTIES.   No. 3 District.

1/9th Bn Argyll & Suthd Highrs.

Regtl.No.	Rank & Name	Casualty.	By Whom Reported.	P.R.
3116.	Pte. Forsyth J.	Killed in Action 10-5-15.	O.C. Battn. 13-7-15.	Nil.
3288.	Pte. Leishman A.	Killed in Action 10-5-15.	O.C. Battn. 13-7-15.	Nil.
2541.	Pte. Gordon J.	Killed in Action 10-5-15.	O.C. Battn. 13-7-15.	Nil.

17-7-15.   J.R.Hood.
                                              Cpl.

To.

   The D.A.AG 2.

      3rd Echelon.
      ───────────

         With reference to the above named. The O.C.
   Battalion states that the Casualties were reported
   by him on 19th May, but were not received by me.
         On receipt of the Army Books 64 I made inquiries
   and the Memo received today dated 13-7-15, states
   that they were Killed in Action 10-5-15.

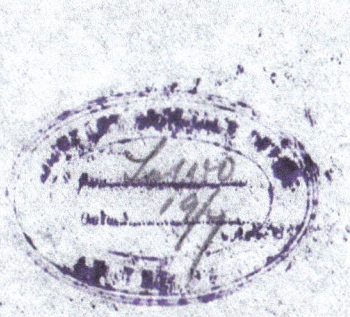

Casualties.   No I District,

1/9th Bn. Argyll &Suthd Highrs.

Regtl. No,	Rank & Name.	Casualty.	By Whom Reported.	P.R.
3359.	Pte. Umpherston A.	Died of Wounds 12-5-15.	O.C.Battn 15-7-15.	W.
1791.	Pte. Brown G.	Missing 10-5-15.	ditto.	N.
1829.	Pte. McVicar J.	Missing 10-5-15.	ditto.	N.
2163.	Pte. Menoch J.	Missing 10-5-15.	ditto,	N.
1384	L/Cpl. Turner D.	Missing 10-5-15.	ditto.	N.
324.	L/Sgt. McAllister A.	Missing 10-5-15-	ditto.	N.
1971.	Pte. McAulay C.	Missing 10-5-15.	ditto.	N.

18-7-15.

CASUALTIES. No 1 District.

1/9th Bn..Argyll & Suthd Highrs.

Regtl. No.	Rank & Name.	Casualty.	By Whom Reported.	P.R. @
2112.	Pte. Docherty E.	Missing. 10-5-15.	O.C. Battn. 7-7-15.	N.

13-7-15.

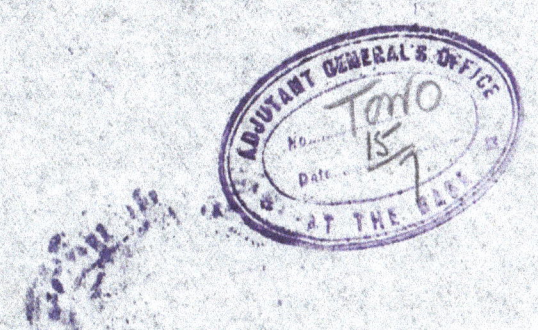

CASUALTIES.   No I District.

1/9th Bn. Argyll & Suthd Highrs.

Regtl. No.	Rank & Name.	Casualty.	By Whom Reported.	P.R.
1767,	Pte. McLean A,	Transferred to England 9-7-15.	A.M.L.O. 9-7-15.	S.
2084.	Pte. Anderson J.	Transferred to England	T.F.Records 15-6-15.	W.

18-7-15.

10th Inf.Bde.
4th Div.

7th BATTN. THE ARGYLL & SUTHERLAND HIGHLANDERS.

A U G U S T

1 9 1 5

7th A & S. Highldrs

WAR DIARY

INTELLIGENCE SUMMARY

Army Form C. 2118.

Hour, Date, Place	Summary of Events and Information	Remarks and References to Appendices
1915 AUGUST 1st to 31st	Battn. in billets at BEAUSSART. Provided working parties daily for R.E.	
AUGUST 11th to 26th	Two platoons in trenches, relieved periodically.	
	The following draft arrived: Aug 5 - 32 O.R. Aug 12 - 110 " Aug 17 - 9 " Aug 24 - 2 Subalterns Aug 25 - 1 "	
	Casualties during August - 3 Men wounded.	

Endcott Lt. Col.
Commanding 7th A & S Hrs

10th Inf.Bde.
4th Div.

7th BATTN. THE ARGYLL & SUTHERLAND HIGHLANDERS.

S E P T E M B E R

1 9 1 5

7TH A. & S. HIGHDRS.

WAR DIARY
INTELLIGENCE SUMMARY
(Erase heading not required.)

Army Form C. 2118.

REF. MAP. AMIENS - SHEET 12.

1915 Hour, Date, Place	Summary of Events and Information	Remarks and References to Appendices
Sept. 1.	Battn. in billets at BEAUSSART.	
Sept. 2. 8 pm.	Moved into Brigade reserve. 1 Coy Colincamps; 1 Coy less 2 Platoons to MAILLY-MAILLET. 2 Platoons (6 second-line Trenches at ELLES SQUARE.	
Sept. 3 to 9.	In Brigade reserve — working parties provided daily.	
Sept. 4.	Reinforcements — 92 N.C.O.'s and men arrived.	
Sept. 9. 8/9 pm	Moved into Divisional reserve at BEAUSSART.	
Sept. 10.	Battn. was reorganized into 4 Companies.	
Sept. 11.	Provided working parties	
„ 12.	do	
„ 13.	do	
„ 14.	do	wounded on fatigue — O.R. 1. (since died of wounds)
„ 15.	Major A.J. McCulloch, 7th D.G. took over command of Battn. Reinforcements 31. O.R. arrived.	
Sept. 16.	Route march; BERTRANGOURT, ACHEUX, FORCEVILLE.	
9. pm.	Moved into Brigade reserve. 1 Coy + H.Q. MAILLY: 1 Coy ELLES SQ.: 2 Coys (less 1 Platoon) COLINCAMPS: 1 Platoon LA SIGNY FARM.	
Sept. 17 5.30 AM	COLINCAMPS billets shelled: O.R. wounded 7. (1 since died of wounds)	
„ 18	Provided working parties.	
„ 19	do	
„ 20	do	
„ 21	do MAILLY billets shelled 1.30 pm. no casualties in this unit	

M.Cullers Major
7th A & S Highrs.

7th A. & S. H. (Cont.)
WAR DIARY
INTELLIGENCE SUMMARY
Army Form C. 2118.

1915 | Hour, Date, Place | Summary of Events and Information | Remarks and references to Appendices

Sept 22 — 7.30 p.m. Battⁿ moved into Divisional Reserve at BEAUSSART.
" 23. Battⁿ (less 1 Coy and M.G. section) moved to 7th Corps Reserve.
H.Q. + 2 Coys to SARTON; 1 Coy to MARIEUX.
1 Coy moved to ACHEUX as 4th Div. Reserve
M.G. Section moved to ACHEUX and remained under to see orders

Sept 24. Companies at SARTON spent cleaning billets and were thoroughly inspected
under Company arrangements. Coy at MARIEUX provided guards and
orderlies at 7 Corps H.Q.

Sept 25 SARTON Coy's route-marched MARIEUX — THIEVRES — ORVILLE.
26 " " " " "
27 " " " " "
28 in billets.   Reinforcements 13 O.R. arrived
29 Company and Battⁿ Training   do.
30   do.   do.
(Including Musk⁶ practice for 2 platoons)

A McCurran Major
O.C. 7 A. & S. Highrs

10th Inf.Bde.
4th Div.

7th BATTN. THE ARGYLL & SUTHERLAND HIGHLANDERS.

O C T O B E R

1 9 1 5

7th A. & S. High.

WAR DIARY
or
INTELLIGENCE SUMMARY

(Erase heading not required.)

Army Form C. 2118.

Ref. Map. AMIENS. Sheet 12.

1915	Hour, Date, Place	Summary of Events and Information	Remarks and references to Appendices
1st Oct.		H.Q. & 2 Coys. Training at SARTON. 1 Coy. providing guards and fatigues at 7th Corps H.Q. MARIEUX. 1 Coy with 4th. Div. at VARENNES. Machine Gun Section in 2nd line Trenches under 10th Inf. Brigade.	
2nd "		do. (Reinforcements 35 O.R. arrived.)	
3rd "		do.	
4th "		do.	
5th "		do.	
6th "	6.30 p.m	Batt'n (less 1 officer and 65 O.R. left at MARIEUX) moved into billets at BEAUSSART rejoining 10th Inf Bde. in divisional reserve.	
7th "		in billets.	
8th "		Provided working parties under 10th Bde. arrangements	
9th "		do	
10th "		do	
11th "		do	
12th "		do	
13th "		Batt'n moved up into Bde Reserve as follows. HQ Machine Guns and A Coy to MAILLY MAILLET. B Coy ELLIS SQUARE C Coy to COLINCAMPS. 1 Platoon C Coy 1 Platoon D Coy to LA SIGNY less 2 platoons to TROSSACHS. 25 O.R. Rejoined D Coy from MARIEUX. 1 platoon D Coy & A Coy relieved detachment D Coy at MARIEUX. (1 Officer 40 O.R.)	
14 —			

T. A. & S. Hqrs.

M'Curson Major
a/ T.A. & S. Hqrs.

WAR DIARY
or
INTELLIGENCE SUMMARY
(Erase heading not required.)

Army Form C. 2118.

Instructions regarding War Diaries and Intelligence Summaries are contained in F. S. Regs., Part II. and the Staff Manual respectively. Title pages will be prepared in manuscript.

Hour, Date, Place	Summary of Events and Information	Remarks and References to Appendices
15 October 1915	Working parties employed at deepening and draining trenches, mending roads and brushing up hedges. TROSSACHS detachment employed on strengthening & clearing up its own trenches which had fallen into disrepair from us having been occupied for two or three months.	
16	Misty day do. Reinforcements 29 O.R. arrived	
17	do	
18	Clear day. Considerable shelling do by enemy. About 30 shells (Maxim Howitzer) fell some 30x in front of TROSSACHS. Enemy hiving munich for on front of continuous rigor of 48 lines, especially on trenches intermeple between Div. 2.30 to 4 owing to the shelling.	
19	Same work do on 16th.	
20	Battn moved back to 4th Divisional Reserve at BEAUSSART.	
21	Bn's Route march via BERTRANCOURT & ACHEUX, ending in a practice attack on return journey.	
22	Working parties employed under Bde arrangements on 1st line trenches & water supply.

7 A. + S. H.

WAR DIARY
or
INTELLIGENCE SUMMARY
(Erase heading not required.)

Army Form C. 2118.

Hour, Date, Place	Summary of Events and Information	Remarks and References to Appendices
23 October 1915	Working parties under Bde arrangements on trenches and water supply.	
24 "	do	
25 "	Batn. was inspected (along with 4th Div.) by His Majesty the King and the President of the French Republic, at ACHEUX.	
26 "	Battalion training in attack.	
27 "	do including point-to-point race via BERTRANCOURT and FOREEVILLE. 3. O.R. arrived.	
28 "	Working parties provided; night parties cancelled owing to bad weather.	
29 "	Working parties provided. night	
30 "	At 6 p.m. Battn moved into trenches between R. Irish Rif. & 11 Tps. on the south and R Dublin Fuseliers & Tps. on the north. Situation of trench line - between BEAUMONT - HAMEL and AUCHONVILLERS. Relief completed by 9 p.m. Capt Seton Browne to Suturative in Rouen. from regn to Lt A R. C. with "D" Coy.	
31 "	All quiet during night. 30. 31st Capt Tomes and Anton arrived as reinforcements. Provided working parties to improvement of his own - trenches very muddy. communications. Capt McCracken arrived as reinforcement.	

M K Cullen Major
O.C 7 A + S H

10th Inf.Bde.
4th Div.

7th BATTN. THE ARGYLL & SUTHERLAND HIGHLANDERS.

N O V E M B E R

1 9 1 5

WAR DIARY
INTELLIGENCE SUMMARY

7th A. & S. High.

Army Form C. 2118.

Ref Map. France 57D.

1915. Hour, Date, Place	Summary of Events and Information	Remarks and references to Appendices
1 November	Enemy very quiet during last 24 hours, except for a sniper from the direction of RAVIN·EN·Y. Found of iron being knocked in heard S. of BEAUMONT-HAMEL about noon. S.E. moderate Transport heard S.E. of BEAUMONT-HAMEL between 5.30 & 7.30 P.M. an explosion was heard N. of RAVIN·EN·Y. about 7 P.M. two Machine Guns sprayed our parapet, but shots were high.	
2 "	Very heavy rain all day, enemy quiet except for intermittent M.G. fire, which did no damage. Our patrols examined the whole of our front line. Wind N.W.	
3 "	Line generally quiet except for a little sniping from BEAUMONT-HAMEL. 5 shells were fired by us about 7.50 A.M. a brow was seen firing N.W. seawards from MIRAUMONT towards PUISIEUX. Horsed transport again heard in BEAUMONT-HAMEL at 7.45 P.M. A German Machine Gun which traversed our parapet at 7.45 P.M. was silenced by our M.G. and has not fired since. Position of German Gun about Q.10.b.7.8. Wind N.W. light. Reinforcements 24. O.R. arriving.	
4 "	Line generally quiet. Horsed transport again heard in BEAUMONT HAMEL at 7.45 P.M. and 1 A.M. Patrols report the Germans working ——— Machine gun active towards our parapet at 4.45 P.M. ——— all night by sap ——— ——— Portion of German gun about Q.10 d.4.8. Wind light N.W.	

J.P.S. Hughes 2/Lt.

Army Form C. 2118.

1/9 A & S Highlanders

WAR DIARY
or
INTELLIGENCE SUMMARY

(Erase heading not required.)

Instructions regarding War Diaries and Intelligence Summaries are contained in F. S. Regs., Part II. and the Staff Manual respectively. Title pages will be prepared in manuscript.

Hour, Date, Place	Summary of Events and Information	Remarks and references to Appendices
5 pm 19/5	Between 5 PM & 11 PM heavy hostile transport entered from S.E. a redoubled enemy Wagons returned in the direction sounds of apparently a steam pump were heard from the direction of RAVIN-EN-Y. Wind NW light. two of our Patrols went within 50 yards of the enemy saps kind While an officer was examining our wire to within 4 unexploded grenades in front of Trench 57 puled up an unexploded German head to enter BEAUMONT HAMEL from the S.E. Hostile transport again was heard working in the direction during the night. steam engine was working near the Railway of RAVIN-EN-Y. M 5 PM a mine was thrown up near at 5.5 PM & 11 PM from the direction Sounds as of blasting were heard	BEAUMONT HAMEL BEAUMONT in the village.
6 pm	of S.E. of BEAUMONT HAMEL. Wind NNE. changed to NW light Very quiet. Hostile transport heard at BEAUMONT HAMEL during the night. Enemy was rather busy in Morning Working Parties could heard as sounds of enemy working parties	Wind light NE changed to N.W.

7th A+S.H.

WAR DIARY
INTELLIGENCE SUMMARY
(Erase heading not required.)

Army Form C. 2118.

Map 57d France

Hour, Date, Place	Summary of Events and Information	Remarks and References to Appendices
1915		
7 Nov. 8 P.M.	Batt. relieved in trenches and went into 4th Div. Reserve at BERTRANCOURT	
8 Nov.	In Billets: Major A.J. McCulloch relinquishes Command on appointment to A.A. + Q.M.G. 2nd Cavalry Div.	
9 Nov.	Supplies working parties under R.A.E. arrangements. Major H.G. Hyslop D.S.O. 2nd A+S.H. assumes Command.	
10 to 13 Nov.	Supplies working parties.	
14 Nov. 7 P.M	Relieved 9th R.I. Rifles in Trenches in front of AUCHONVILLERS.	
15 Nov.	Enemy very quiet: 3 – 5.30 P.M. carried out practice in Artillery Barrage arrangement. Grenadiers under Lieut Lockhart at 11.30 A.M. Enemy set free a pig from which flew direct, N.W. Unusually heavy movement of transport heard at 9.15 P.M. just N.E. of BEAUMONT. Enemy busy sandbagging their trenches, our German snipers rather active but firing high during 11 Stokes.	
16 Nov.	Enemy working party (20 men) 10.30 A.M. behind their trench Q.5.a. dispersed with rifle fire. A little sniping, otherwise enemy very quiet. About 6.30 A.M. enemy sent over 11 whiz-bangs, but did no damage. Return 11 & 12 noon from Gun N of BEAUMONT 7.30 A.M. scatters by rifle-fire.	
17 Nov.	Our guns shelled BEAUMONT and a few whiz-bangs came in retaliation. 1.35 to 1.40 P.M. dense column of black smoke seen 72 degrees E of true North from Q.10, apparently about ½ mile away. Enemy working and whiz bang between BEAUMONT and RAVIN. En Y. 4 whiz-bangs heavy working behind front trench. at 9 P.M. and did no damage. At 9.30 P.M. slight enemy transport heard E of BEAUMONT	H.G Hyslop Major Commanding 7th A+S.H.

7th A. & S. Highrs.

Army Form C. 2118.

WAR DIARY
or
INTELLIGENCE SUMMARY
(Erase heading not required.)

1915 Hour, Date, Place	Summary of Events and Information	Remarks and References to Appendices
November 17	About 7.15 P.M. a party of Germans, three or bombing apparently in trench 59, threw burst in our wire; sentries opened fire and shouts were heard. Red flares were used by enemy immediately after, and heavy bursts of machine-gun fire swept our parapet accurately.	at SAP
18	Enemy very quiet during the day – Batt. was relieved at 8. P.M by 9th R.I. Fusiliers, and proceeded to billets in MAILLY.	
19	In billets. Furnished 100 men as working party, for R.E.	
20	Moved to 4th Div. reserve in billets at BEAUSSART. 6.15. P.M.	
21	In billets. Cleaning clothes and equipment	
22	" " Company training, and work on improvement of trenches. Reinforcements 25. O.R. arrived also (men?) working party of 100 for Grenade School
23	" "	
24	" "	
25	" "	
26	Moved into 10 Bde reserve: H.Q. + 1 Coy MAILLY. 1 Coy. ELLES SQ (with 2. M.G.). 2 Coys (Gen 1 (Maton) COLINCAMPS: 1 Platoon LA SIGNY.	
27/31	Provides working parties for R.E. under R.E. arrangements.	

H.G. Hyslop Lt Col
Cmdg 7th Argyll & Sutherland Highlanders

10th Inf.Bde.
4th Div.

7th BATTN. THE ARGYLL & SUTHERLAND HIGHLANDERS.

D E C E M B E R

1 9 1 5

Army Form C. 2118.

7th Argyll & Sutherland High'rs

WAR DIARY
or
INTELLIGENCE SUMMARY
(Erase heading not required.)

Instructions regarding War Diaries and Intelligence Summaries are contained in F. S. Regs., Part II. and the Staff Manual respectively. Title pages will be prepared in manuscript.

Hour, Date, Place	Summary of Events and Information	Remarks and references to Appendices
1915 December 1	In 10th Bde Reserve: Provided working parties for R.E.	
2. 1.30 am	Moved into 4th Div. Reserve at BEAUSSART.	
3.	In billets cleaning and drying clothes and equipment. Provided working parties for R.E. 4 Lewis Guns received 3/12/15	
4/7		
8.	Moved into 10th Bde Reserve: HQ. + 1 Coy MAILLY. 1 Coy. ELES SQ. 2 Coys (less 1 Platoon) COLINCAMPS: 1 Platoon LA SIGNY. 4 Machine Guns in front line with 8th Royal Irish Rifles.	
9. 6 to 9 p.m.	Attempt to light shell fires into COLINCAMPS were killed, but no damage done. Provided working parties for R.E. from COLINCAMPS + MAILLY.	
10/12	Provided working parties for R.E.	
13. 6.30	Moved into 4th Div. Reserve at BEAUSSART	
14	In billets cleaning clothes and equipment	
15/16	Provided working parties for R.E.	
17. 5.pm.	Relieved 9th R.I. Rifles in trenches at Q.10 -(Sheet 57D. FRANCE) less 2 Machine Guns at ELES SQUARE (Q.33) and 1 Platoon AUCHONVILLERS.	
18.	About 16 Field gun shells were fired into AUCHONVILLERS at 11.45 am, and the same number at 12.10 p.m. Otherwise a quiet day. Reinforcements in D.R. arrived.	
19.	Everything quiet: enemy busy draining their trenches	

Page 2

● 7th Argyll + Sutherland ● Hypln—

WAR DIARY
or
INTELLIGENCE SUMMARY
(Erase heading not required.)

Army Form C. 2118.

Instructions regarding War Diaries and Intelligence Summaries are contained in F. S. Regs., Part II. and the Staff Manual respectively. Title pages will be prepared in manuscript.

Hour, Date, Place	Summary of Events and Information	Remarks and references to Appendices
1915		
December 20.	About 11.30 A.m. our left sector was shelled with 75 to 30 light fired singly. Shooting was accurate but little damage done - no casualties.	Shrapnel and H.E. no casualties.
21.	a quiet day, except for a few shells fired on ground at 11.45 A.M. - 7 P.M. relieved by 8th R.I.R. was proceeded to 4th Div. Reserve.	E at BUCQUOY ERS To Billets at BEAUSSART
22	Cleaning clothes and equipment.	
23/24	Provided working parties for R.E.	
25	In Billets	
26/31	Provided working parties for R.E.	

[signatures]
Lt Col
7th Argyll Hyp

4th Division

10th Infantry Bde.

7th & 9th Battn Argyll & Sutherland
           Highlanders

✗ 9 BN FROM 27 DIV. 81 BDE amalgamated with 7 BN May 15

~~J...y Transport~~

~~11th~~

~~Feb 1916~~

1914 DEC — 1915 JUN

1.L.

$\frac{121}{3871}$

Army Book 153.

7th Argyll & Sutherland H^{rs}

Vol I. 1 – 31.12.14

Army Form C. 2118.

WAR DIARY
~~INTELLIGENCE~~ SUMMARY

7th Battn. Argyll Highlanders and Sutherland Highlanders

Hour, Date, Place	Summary of Events and Information	Remarks and references to Appendices
1914 December 1 – 11	At BEDFORD hutted. Battalion training	
11	Moved to SOUTHAMPTON	
12, 13, 14	At Southampton – Inspection and fitting out – Route marching	
15	Left Southampton by "P.O. Tintoretto" for HAVRE	
16, 17, 18 & 19	At HAVRE – Inspection and fitting out – Route marching	
19/20	Left HAVRE and arrived at St OMER. thence to HELFAUT and BILQUES	
20/31	At HELFAUT and BILQUES – daily practice in Battalion training and Musketry with the C.L.I.E. magazine Rifle MkI*	

HELFAUT
31.12.14

James Carney /Lt Colonel/
Comdg 7th Battn A.& S. Highrs

10th Inf.Bde.
4th Div.

Battn. joined Bde.
on 6.1.15 from
Army Troops.

7th BATTN. THE ARGYLL & SUTHERLAND HIGHLANDERS.

J A N U A R Y

1 9 1 5

7th Battalion Argyll & Sutherland Highlanders

Army Form C. 2118.

WAR DIARY
~~INTELLIGENCE~~ SUMMARY
(Erase heading not required.)

Instructions regarding War Diaries and Intelligence Summaries are contained in F. S. Regs., Part II. and the Staff Manual respectively. Title pages will be prepared in manuscript.

Hour, Date, Place	Summary of Events and Information	Remarks and References to Appendices
1915 January 1 — 3	At HELFAUT – Practice Battalion Training	
4	At HAZEBROUCK – as right	
5	At BAILLEUL	
6	At NIEPPE	
7 – 9	8 Officers and 76 N.C.Os in Trenches each day for 24 hours. Remainder Company training	
10 – 13	Each Double Company in Trenches for 24 hours at a time distributed among the men in the Trenches. – Remainder Company Training	
14 – 17	Each Double Company in Trenches for 24 hours at a time – As sections – Remainder Company Training	
18 – 21	Each Double Company in Trenches for 24 hours at a time – As platoons – under Platoon Commanders – Remainder Company Training	
22 – 23	Company Training	
24 – 31	Each Double Company in Trenches for 48 hours – As Platoons under Platoon Commanders. Remainder Company Training	

ARMENTIÈRES
31.1.15

James Clark (Lt Colonel)
Comdg 7th Battn A & S Hrs

10th Inf.Bde.
4th Div.

7th BATTN. THE ARGYLL & SUTHERLAND HIGHLANDERS.

F E B R U A R Y

1 9 1 5

Army Form C. 2118.

WAR DIARY
or
INTELLIGENCE SUMMARY

7th Battalion Acting as (Red Cross) attached to 1st Highlanders

Hour, Date, Place	Summary of Events and Information	Remarks and references to Appendices
1915 February 1st – 3rd	Two Companies in the Trenches each for 48 hours 40 Platoons under Platoon Commanders. Remaining two Companies Company training	
4th – 12th	Two Companies in the Trenches each for four days and each in a different section. Remaining two Companies Company training Musketry. Instruction in use of Short Rifle, Grenade throwing, Range finding &c.	
13th – 28th	Two Companies in the Trenches for four days. One to a section of the line and the other in Brigade Reserve. The two Companies not in the Trenches Company training, Musketry, Grenade throwing &c.	

Casualties in Trenches during Month from 1st to 23rd February inclusive

	Killed	Died of Wounds	Wounded	Missing	Total
Officers	nil	nil	nil	nil	Total nil
Other Ranks	1	1	5	nil	Total 7

ARMENTIÈRES
28. 2. 15

James Cuninghame Lt Colonel
Comdg 7th Battn A. & S. H.

10th Inf.Bde.
4th Div.

7th BATTN. THE ARGYLL & SUTHERLAND HIGHLANDERS.

M A R C H

1 9 1 5

WAR DIARY
INTELLIGENCE SUMMARY

1st Bn. Argyll & Suth'land High'rs

Hour, Date, Place	Summary of Events and Information	Remarks and references to Appendices
March 1st to 14th	Two Companies always on duty in the trenches, of these one held the right of the DOUVE sector, the other being in reserve. Two Companies in Billets at ARMENTIÈRES. The Companies in trenches were relieved every four days.	Map 28 (YPRES)
14th – 17th	On the night of 14th March the Companies in the trenches were relieved by the Welsh Rgt, and rejoined Head Quarters at ARMENTIÈRES with a view to taking over trenches held by 17th & 18th B'de South of the River LYS	MAP. 36 (LILLE)
17th – 22nd 19th	On 19th March the Batt'n took over again the line that had been formerly held and on 19th Headquarters & two Companies moved to the PIGGERIES and GRANDE MUNQUE FME (T.M.4.)	MAP. 28 (YPRES)
22nd – 30th	On 22nd March two Companies occupied the trenches forming the Right Sector of the line occupied by the 10th Inf. Bd 15 oct, with 2 frontage of about 800 yds. These Companies are relieved by those in billets every 4th day.	

LA GRANDE MUNQUE F'me
30. 3. 13. —

Casualties 1st Feb. 29th March
Killed   wounded   Total
Other Ranks   3   4   7.

Alex Rankin Lt Col
Com'g 1st Bn. Argyll & Suth'land High'rs

10th Inf.Bde.
4th Div.

7th BATTN. THE ARGYLL & SUTHERLAND HIGHLANDERS.

A P R I L

1 9 1 5

WAR DIARY or INTELLIGENCE SUMMARY

(Erase heading not required.) 7th A. & S. Highrs Also

Army Form C. 2118.

REF. MAP Sheet 28 YPRES

Hour, Date, Place	Summary of Events and Information	Remarks and references to Appendices
1st Apl – 17th Apl	Headquarters remained at PICQERIES & LA GRANDE Hq Companies in trenches two in Billets. The Battn was relieved by 4th Oxfords handing over Billets in the vicinity. The Battn moved into Billets having and trenches in the vicinity. The Battn moved into Billets to not about 2 miles to 9 BAILLEUL [where the remainder of the Brigade was quartered] Hqrs. The Battn remained in the above Billets	MARQUE FARM
18th Apl – 23rd Apl	The Battn remained in the above Billets	
23rd "	Orders on recent eveng The Bn to be ready to move from at short notice and at 1.40pm the Battn paraded and marched on BAILLEUL to LOCRE where they arrived about 11.30pm & billeted for the night. heard from LOCRE at 1 am about 5 miles to OUDERDOM into huts. acc packs were left here also 3 wd Line transport rly NAA Tpt & mach. gun limber accompany of the Battn when transport was continued at 5 pm. A halt was made at Gpn about 1 mile E of ST JEAN – YPRES.	
25th "	Shortly after midnight the march was continued to ST JEAN to WIELTJE where a halt was made about 2 am and wilding for the operations issued. The Bn was to form a support to R Irish Regt the orders being to attack over C 10 x 11 forming up with the left on line W10.6.6 to 10.4 to 10 to from in line of them for the remaining Battns in the Bgde Q.I. Irish & R.Dubs the run is to attack ST JULIEN advance of to East & West of the ST JULIEN - FORTUIN Rd respectively formed up by Hqrd was of 2/5 the R.Dubs Rgts 2 Battns FUSILIERS RAJO. A.S.H.	

WAR DIARY or INTELLIGENCE SUMMARY

Army Form C. 2118

(Erase heading not required.) 1 – A old Hythe

Hour, Date, Place	Summary of Events and Information	Remarks and references to Appendices
25 Sept (Sat 5) 4.30 a.m.	The B'fast came under fire on reaching C.23.C. roll. The R. War. Reg? had been told to form for attack facing in 16. Lands? to the enemy. A good few casualties occurred here. A Coy moved to the S.E. corner of C.17.C. followed by B Coy to reach that point. They had reached ground except for rifle & m.g. fire from a number asking for reinforcements, on his left being received from the R. War. Reg?. A Coy must form in three lines the second in waves and carried by a heavy fire from them succeeded in working their way up to the triangle of trees in that the firing line B Coy was moved under cover not to the East and forward up to the triangle of trees in that front of C.17.C from which point it was seen to get reinforcements up to the firing line. C & B Coys were directed on this point. The Batt? became a good deal mixed here with the Scottish & some of the R. War. Reg? and the principle counter occurred he not up where the Close after this but no any heavy shelled by H.E. lyds from Reinforcements were sent forward the there capture taken sufficing but that the first line was written down and a position taken up further from N point of farm in C.23.b this farm in C.17.C. to form in C.17.d. thence E to stream in C.17.C. There was no preliminary bombardment, a few shells only being dropped in the wood, the farms on which the R. War. Reg? and Norfolk field H.Q. Each was found to be in the enemys hands & full M.G. fire	

Army Form C. 2118.

WAR DIARY
or
INTELLIGENCE SUMMARY
(Erase heading not required.) 7th Bn. 1st Sigh. Bde

Instructions regarding War Diaries and Intelligence Summaries are contained in F. S. Regs., Part II. and the Staff Manual respectively. Title pages will be prepared in manuscript.

Hour, Date, Place	Summary of Events and Information	Remarks and references to Appendices
25th Ap.l (Cont'd)	The Canadians the men on our left might have cooperated but were not aware any attack was going to be made. The regt? remained in its position & had taken up their posts and the Reserve & no counter attack was made on them. Casualties roughly amounted to Officers killed 6 wounded 6 missing nil Other Ranks " 100 " 170 " 150 a large number of the missing having fortunately been slightly wounded and have since but other missing stations & some men having attacked Keerselare to the North. After dark the regiment took up a position in trenches South of farm	G.8.T. 21.8 1st Can Div
26th Ap.l	Remained in above trenches which was shelled All during the morning to the just N of this farm	
27th - 28 Ap.l	Remained in above trenches. On 27th supported attack by Srn.nd B.P. on our left. Brought down an enemy aeroplane in our lines on 28th During these days the trenches were continually shelled by heavy guns the trenches being blown in in many places. The Bn. Q. Duffield Kev. Carnochan on the night of 2nd Bat. man who was hit by Lanc. Fus. and more took their support trenches C. 21 about ½ a mile. Me Gordon H.Q.t. On 27 2nd Highlrs

10th Inf Bde
4th Div.

7th BATTN. THE ARGYLL & SUTHERLAND HIGHLANDERS

MAY

1 9 1 5

(Note: The 7th & 9th Battns. The
Argyll & Sutherlands
were organized as a Composite
Battalion on 29.5.15.
Independant formations were
resumed on 20.7.15, the 9th
Battn being transfered to Vl.
Corps as Corps Troops.)

Attached:

Account of Action
24th May
Casualty Lists.

WAR DIARY
or
INTELLIGENCE SUMMARY
(Erase heading not required.)

7th A. & S. Highlanders

Ref. Map. Sheet 28 YPRES

Army Form C. 2118.

Hour, Date, Place	Summary of Events and Information	Remarks and references to Appendices
May 1st	10ᵗʰ in support trenches C.21.d about 200 ʸᵈˢ near Ypres from Chev Badly shelled by Maxy [?] guns during afternoon and three 9 [?] Crewithas [?]	
2nd	Same trenches. During a day the mind [?] being favorable to the enemy used 2 lot of asphyxiating gases to copie [?] us attack a Battn of 15. 8ᵗʰ K.O.S.B. in our immediate company trench in C.16.a in M seen to be leaving their trench and retiring. It was found that the trenches in front of us had been occupied by the enemy we opened fire on them and stopped an advance. Shortly afterwards a Batter of R.F. to our left in parr [?] in the trench by this time some army of the Brick fields which was masked by that grove [?] and shot was marked by the brigade to arms [?] from the support line, very quietly occupied the trench, and some men were sent upon [?] to [?] effect of the fires and reinforce	
3rd	our splinter advanced in their attempts to suppose [?] from Brigade & some in the trenches lately taken up and from 6 am onwards [?] shelled and an attack was expected 6 am very heavy shelling [?] even my [?] to a company front about 3 am Lieut Colling [?] others about 2 am when coming again shells [?] to keep Trench 2. 10 10 am was relieved by relief [?] and moved to	

1247 W 3299 200,000 (E) 8/14 J.B.C. & A. Forms/C. 2118/11.

WAR DIARY
or
INTELLIGENCE SUMMARY

(Erase heading not required.)

Army Form C. 2118.

Hour, Date, Place	Summary of Events and Information	Remarks and references to Appendices

4/5 – 6/5 Remained in trenches in C.20.C. and was occasionally slightly shelled. Moved to B CROUCILLES.

7/6 Moved during the night from the trench to C.35.a.

8/7 Got badly shelled by hvy heavy guns during the night and had to shift from the S. along the CANAL BANK at 8 p.m. where a new mon [?] LA BRIQUE (C.28.a) in support of 13.F.Bde. Came under shell fire at 10 p.m. & suffered casualties. Bn has and suffering in S.W. of YPRES-LANGEMARK Rd. the line running NN/E from Pt. 18 a. 275 - ST JEAN Rd. from about 300 y. The Bn.H.Q.R.E. advanced to attack at 11a/15 - ST JEAN Rd from men in left in line of advance & being on right of 1 Bt. R. Irish in new line of advance — the from O.21.d (Roule) on WIELTJE Road was put at the right & this flank had no enemy troops forward in WIELTJE or S. of it. The Regt was withdrawn at dawn N. of the Canal. The Casualties. The day were: Officers (2 LKGunners) killed and 3m o. Ranks killed & wounded.

9/6 – 12/5 En. huts in H.11.d & mens tents here had a much needed rest. Kit was done by the Batt. Laundry. The great fatigues have been repeated herein most favorably commented upon by various commanders. The Brig. R.

WAR DIARY
or
INTELLIGENCE SUMMARY

Army Form C. 2118.

Hour, Date, Place	Summary of Events and Information	Remarks and references to Appendices
12th	The Batt'n moved leaving 1/2 afternoon via Brielen by tram from [illegible]	
13th	Moved in A.23.d. to billets from Tram Hour on the road [illegible] over 10th used	
	Battalion [illegible] in Billets in Tram House in A.23.d.	
14th	In the evening the Batt'n moved to billets in VLAMERTINGHE.	
15th	Col 7pm the Batt'n moved to Dug Outs at Canal Bank	
	No 2 Pontoon Bridge	
16th	The Battalion moved to Duff's Trenches at ST JEAN at C.28.a.	
	1 Killed, 2 wounded	
17th–18th	The Batt'n still occupied same trenches. Heavy shelling by	
	Enemy. 1 killed, 5 wounded	
18th–19th	Moved back to Reserve at [illegible] Redoubt at LA BRIGUE	
20th	The Batt'n move back to Canal Bank No 2 Pontoon Bridge	
21st	Still at Canal Bank. At 7pm 1/2 of 21st the Battalion	
	moved up to Duff at trenches at WELTJE, relieving	
	the 2nd Seaforths	
22nd	The Battalion occupied Duff's trenches at WELTJE another	
	heavy day's shelling [Thereupon being actively] on the	
	night of 22nd moved forward to Fitzcy Drive	
23rd	Remained there on Sunday 23rd. 2 Killed, 2 wounded	

WAR DIARY
or
INTELLIGENCE SUMMARY
(Erase heading not required.)

Army Form C. 2118.

Hour, Date, Place	Summary of Events and Information	Remarks and references to Appendices
24th	At 3 a.m. on 24th while hilly the Enemy suddenly attacked our Battalion suffering very heavily nearly 200 just in front of the trenches were twenty killed out right, 2 officers killed (2 Lieuts Shaw & Smith) 6 men killed, 9 officers wounded & 199 men wounded. On the night of 24th the Battalion were relieved & withdrew to the Day huts at Camil Bank & the 2 Batt'y Bgde.	
25th	On arrival of 25th the Batt. (6 officers & 84 men) moved to Zonnebeke billet A.26 where they remained on A.26 and rested.	
26th 27th 28th	Remained in Billets at Zonnebeke	
29th	at 4 p.m. when they marched to Billets A.16th along with the 9 Lancs (3 officers 131 men)	
30th	On morning 29th Major Solater R.I.F. arrived from 4th Divn to reorganize & take command of 7th & 9th Argylls. The Argyleshire was duly reorganized. The surplus officers & three returned to 9 Argylls at Zonnebeke. Work of Organization proceeded. Battalion was visited by Brigadier General & General Commanding 9 Divn	
31st	Battalion still in Billets at Farm A.16.c	

J. Lewis, Captain
7th Argylls

ACCOUNT OF ACTION 24TH MAY.

P.P. with War Diary.

Copy.   Drill Princes Street, Stirling.
11th August 1925.

The Historical Section (Military Branch)

Dear Sir,

<u>7th Battn. Argyll and Sutherland Highlanders.</u>

Reference my letter of 24th June 1925, I enclose herewith accounts by Major W. McCracken, D.S.O., T.D. and Lieut.-Colonel J.M. Scott, D.S.O., and also an envelope and message which have been retained as a memento of the occasion.

Would you kindly let me have this latter back when you are finished with it.

I am sorry there has been such delay, but I have been unable to obtain the accounts sooner.

Yours faithfully,

C.B. Robertson, Capt. and Adj.
for Lieut.-Col. comdg. 7/Argyll and S. Hrs.

Major W. McCracken's Account.

The 7th Argyll and Sutherland Hrs. under command of Lieut.-Colonel Carden relieved the 1/ Warwickshire in the front line extending from Wieltje - St. Julien road to the south for about 400 yards. The 2nd Dublin Fusiliers were on the left, and the 1st Royal Scots Fusiliers on the right The relief was completed at about 1 a.m. on 24th May. The 7/Argyll had the 5th Border Regiment mixed through them for instruction and about half the strength of the 7/Argyll mentioned would consist of 5th Border Regiment N.C.O's and men. I was in command of D coy on the right of 7/Argyll. At dawn or about 2.15 a.m. gas from enemies trenches some 150 yards off was distinctly heard blowing out of cylinders and reached our line in a few seconds. This was accompanied by a very heavy bombardment which was kept up for many hours. The enemy did not reach our trenches unless temporarily on our extreme left, where the unit on our left had been overpowered. Many of our newly arrived men went back from our line when the gas attack began, but the majority put up a good fight and held the line, although the casualties were very heavy. In the forenoon Colonel Carden sent me back to La Brique for our M.O., as we had so many badly wounded officers and men in the front line, which was very broken and irregular, and its location probably unknown to the M.O. I came back with out M.O. and also a company (B under Capt. Paterson) of 2/Seaforth, who reinforced the whole 7/Argyll line and made it quite well held. The casualties from shell fire had continued all day, however, so much so that before I was sent to hospital in the afternoon from effects of gas onoy 4 out of about 24 officers were left.
Of these Lt.-Col. J.M. Scott was senior, and if further information is required, as he took over command after the battalion was relieved on the evening of 24th May, he will be able to furnish all particulars.

Lieut.-Colonel J.M. Scott's Account.

With reference to the battalion's action on 24th May 1915, I agree with the details as set down by Major McCracken, and can add very little to the narrative.

We held the front line trench all day, with the assistance of D Coy. 2/Seaforth, and after dusk the brigadier sent for me to attend a conference in a house in St. Jean. There I received instructions to prepare for withdrawal from the front line, under cover of troops, who were digging a new line about 300 yards to our rear. This plan was necessary owing to our left flank being in the air. The front and support trench, originally held by the 2/Dublin Fusiliers to the north of Wieltje - St. Julien road, having been captured and retained by the enemy.

In the early hours of the morning 25th May, just before dawn and after out wounded had been cleared and the trench partially filled in, we evacuated the front line, and withdrew through the covering troops to the canal bank, where we reorganized and remained in reserve until the Brigade was relieved.

The casualties were excessive, owing to the accurate and very heavy fire, which appeared to take our line in enfilade. The line was also in my opinion too thickly held on the morning of 24th May; the number of officers to men being out of all proportion. Many casualties were caused amongst the men who retired at the first appearance of the chlorine gas; not only did they become further gassed by moving with the cloud, but they also ran into the enemy's barrage which lifted from our front line to the support line immediately prior to their infantry assault. The men of the old 7th were very steady and did excellent work under most trying conditions.

Unfortunately the records of messages and orders given or received, were lost when the Adjutant Major Campbell went down badly gassed.

Pencil note on back of old envelope.

Reinforcements wanted where C Company 7/Argyles were posted last night, ie. right of road.

        Arthur B. Cowburn,
                Capt. 5/Border

24/5/15.
2 p.m.

I am senior officer present. Men steady but sparsely placed along trench. Casualties fairly high.

Colonel Sir Philip Trotter forwards the enclosed papers relating to the gallant conduct of the 7th battalion on 24th May and which he has just received from the front.

Stirling Carter,
4th June 1915.

Copy.

O.C. Depot, Argyle and Sutherland Highlanders.

G.485   25th May 1915.

    The attached envelope and message have been sent in here by 85th Bde. and I am forwarding them to you by the desire of General Wilson commanding 4th Division as a memento of the most gallant defence made by the 7th Bn. Argyle and Sutherland Highlanders on 24th May. Although badly gassed at dawn and heavily shelled all day they hung on to their part of the line even after the Germans had broken through on their left. They proved themselves in every way worthy of the very high reputation they have won since joining this division.

                                            C. Garsia.
                                                Capt. G.S.
                                                    4th Division.

Copy.
 4th Division.
G.L. 896   24th

Attached forwarded for your information.

From 28th Division.
4.40 p.m.   Loch,
                                  Lieut.-Col.

Copy.

To 28th Division.

B.M. 181.   24th.

A torn piece of paper taken off a sick man here has following on it begins aaa. Reinforcements wanted where C Company 7/Argyles were posted last night i.e. right of road signed A.B. Cowburn Captain 5 Borders ends aaa do not know to which brigade these units belong aaa Your G.L. 889 received.

85th Inf. Bde.
3.50 p.m.

O.C. Administrative Centre,
  7/Argyll and Sutherland Highlanders.

Officer Commanding,
2/7th A. & S. Highlanders, Hawick.

    I beg to acknowledge having received correspondence forwarded by you, and which was sent to Colonel Sir Philip Trotter, O.C. Depot A. & S.H. Stirling.

    I shall see that same is carefully preserved.

        H.S. Captain,
            O.C. Admin. Centre,
                7/A. and S. Highlanders.

2/7th Arg. and Suth'd. Hrs.
Orderly Room 7th June 1915
No. 290.

Officer Commanding,
    Administrative Centre,
        7th A. & S. Highlanders,
            Alloa.

    The enclosed correspondence has been ~~receive~~ forwarded to me by Sir Philip Trotter, commanding the Depot, A. & S.H. to whom it had been sent in error.

    Before sending it to you for preservation, I have published an extract of it in battalion orders (see No. 129/15 para. 1052).

                          Alex. Black, for O.C.
                          Capt. and Adj. 2/& A. and S. Hrs.

Hawick,
7.6.15.

CASUALTY LISTS.

Casualty Report.   No.1 District.

1/9th Battn: Argyll & Suthd: Hrs.

Regtl.No. Rank & Name.	Casualty.	Reptd. by	Prev. Report
2526 Pte. Duffy J.J.	INFLUENZA. Adm. 85th Field Amb. 5/4/15.	O.C. 85th Field Ambulance	Nil.
1925 Pte. McEwan F.	G.S.W. HEAD. DIED OF WOUNDS 25/4/15.	O.C. No.5 C.C. Station	Nil.
2491 Pte. Buchanan C.	TO DUTY, 11/4/15.	O.C. Conv. Depot.	S.
2128 Pte. Young J.	TO DUTY, 28/4/15.	,,	S.
1988 Pte. Lawrence C.	TO DUTY, 30/4/15.	,,	W.
2160 Pte. Sinclair J.	TO DUTY, 30/4/15.	,,	W.

3rd Echelon,   Captain, for
4/5/15.   Officer Commanding, T.F. Infantry Records

Casualty Report.   No. 1 District.
1/9th Battn: Argyll & Suthd. Hrs.

Regtl. No.	Rank & Name.		Casualty.	Reptd. by & Date.	Prev. Rpt
1529	Pte. Stevenson	J.	TO DUTY 1/5/15.	O.C. Conv. Depot 1/5/15.	W.
1651	,, Millar	T.	TO DUTY 1/5/15.	,,	W.
2672	,, Todd	A.	TO DUTY 1/5/15.	,,	S.
1461	,, Ward	F.	SPRAINED R.ANKLE, Adm. 83rd F.Amb. 19/4/15.	O.C. 83rd F.Amb. 25/4/15.	Nil.
1596	,, Fleming	D.	NEURALGIA, Adm. 83rd F.Amb. 23/4/15.	,,	Nil.
2721	,, Bissett	W.	SCALDED FOOT Adm. 83rd F.Amb. 23/4/15.	,,	Nil.
2247	,, McKinnon	J.	ABCESS, R.WRIST, Adm. 83rd F.Amb. 19/4/15.	,,	Nil.
2261	Sergt. Johnstone	W.G.	HERNIA. Adm. 83rd Field Amb. 22/4/15.	,,	Nil.
2500	,, Blair	J.	TONSILITIS, Adm. 83rd F.Amb. 23/4/15.	,,	Nil.
2682	Pte. White	J.	DYSPEPSIA, Adm. 83rd F.Amb. 23/4/15.	,,	Nil.
5033	Pte. Cameron	D.	RHEUMATISM, Adm. 83rd F.Amb. 22/4/15.	,,	Nil.
1457	Sgt. Ablett	R.	TO DUTY. 5/5/15.	O.C. Conv. Depot. 5/5/15.	W.
1543	Pte Pratt	J.	KILLED IN ACTION 13/4/15.	O.C. Battn: 24/4/15.	Nil.
1925	,, McEwan	F.	KILLED IN ACTION 25/4/15.	O.C. No.5 C.C.Stn. 29/4/15.	Nil.
1852	,, Howie	W.	KILLED IN ACTION 23/4/15.	O.C. Battn: 1/5/15.	Nil.
1580	,, Mulgrew	K.	KILLED IN ACTION 24/4/15.	,,	Nil.
1722	,, Healey	J.	KILLED IN ACTION 27/4/15.	,,	Nil.
1611	,, SCOTT	J.F.	KILLED IN ACTION 28/4/15.	,,	Nil.

3rd Echelon,
11/5/15.

Captain, for
Officer I/C T.F. Infantry Rcds.

Casualties   1/9th Battn. Argyll & Suthd. Hrs.   No.1 District.

Regtl.No. Rank & Name	Casualty	By whom repotd.. date	Prev.Rpt.
2571 Pte Kennedy D.	TO ENGLAND, 4/5/15.	O&C.Rainfcets.4/5/15.	Nil.
2523 ,, Drummond J.	TO ENGLAND, 4/5/15.	,,	,,
1568 ,, McNeill D.	TO ENGLAND, 4/5/15.	,,	,,
2491 ,, Buchanan C.	TO ENGLAND, 4/5/15.	,,	,,
2611 ,, McKendrick J.D.	TO DUTY, 6/5/15.	O.C.Conv.Depot,6/5/15.	W.
1457 Cpl. Ablett R.	TO DUTY, 5/5/15.	,,	W.
Lieut. Forster F.N.	WOUNDED, 9/5/15.	O.C.Battalion	Nil.

3rd Echelon, G.H.Q.,
12/5/15.

HCodrington   Captain, for
Officer I/C T.F.Infantry Records.

Casualties.   No. 1 District.

1/7th. Bn. The Argyll & Sutherland Highlanders.

Rank & Name	Casualty	Rpd. by.	Prev. Rpd. Casualty.
Lieut. Col. Clark James G.B.	KILLED IN ACTION. 10/5/15.	O.C. Batt.	Nil.
Lieut. Hutton F.R.H.	KILLED IN ACTION. 10/5/15.	O.C. Batt.	Nil.
2/Lieut. Campbell K.J.	KILLED IN ACTION. 10/5/15.	O.C. Batt.	Nil.
2/Lieut. Birrell G.H.	KILLED IN ACTION. 10/5/15.	O.C. Batt.	Nil.

Captain for,
O. I/c. Terr. Infantry Records, 3rd. Echelon, G.H.Q.
3rd. Echelon, General Headquarters, 16th. May 1915.

Casualties.

No. 1 District.

1/9th. Bn. The Argyll & Sutherland Higherlanders.

Regt. No.	Rank & Name.	Casualty.	Rpd. By	Prev. Rpd. Casualty.
	2/Lieut. Prior C. C.	WOUNDED IN ACTION. 10/5/15.	D.C. Batt.	Nil.
1294	S.M. Whelan F. W.	SHOCK. Ad. 1 Can. F.A. 24/4/15.	O.C. No. 1. Can. F.A.	Nil.
3051	L.Cpl. Ferns J.	To Duty 12/5/15.	Con. Dpt. Rouen.	W.
1939	Pte. Cameron E.	G.S.W. ABDOMEN. DIED FROM WOUNDS 5/5/15.	O.C. No.2 C.Hospl.	Nil.
2636	Pte. Petrie A.	To Duty 15/5/15.	O.C. Con.D. Rouen	W.
2537	Pte. Gillies A.	To Duty 9/5/15.	do.	S.W.
2557	L.Cpl Hood A.	To Duty 13/5/15.	do.	W.

Capt. for,
O.i/c. Terr. Infantry Records, 3rd. Echelon,
G.H.Q. 18/5/15.

CASUALTY REPORT. MAY 20th. 1915.

1/7th. Argyll & Sutherland Hghlds.

Regtl. No.	Rank	Name		CASUALTY.		P.R.
1630	Cpl.	Johnston	W.	KILLED IN ACTION.	10-5-15.	Nil.
2134	Pte.	Bauld	J.	" " "	10-5-15.	Nil.
2494	"	Brown	T.	" " "	10-5-15.	Nil.
2543	"	Green	R.	" " "	10-5-15.	Nil.
1805	"	McKinnon	G.	" " "	8-5-15.	Nil.
2481	"	Aitken	R.	" " "	8-5-15.	Nil.
1421	"	Gray	W.	" " "	9-5-15.	Nil.
2478	"	Kennedy	M.	" " "	9-5-15.	Nil.
2865	"	Lambert	P.	" " "	9-5-15.	Nil.
2584	"	Monoghan	V.	" " "	9-5-15.	Nil.
3265	"	McKendrick	T.	" " "	9-5-15.	Nil.
2499	"	Black	R.	" " "	10-5-15.	Nil.
2441	"	Letters	D.	" " "	10-5-15.	Nil.
2634	"	Pennan	S.	" " "	10-5-15.	Nil.
2740	"	Shields	J.	" " "	10-5-15.	Nil.
2613	L/C.	McGeachy	G.	" " "	10-5-15.	Nil.
2484	Pte.	Adam	W.	" " "	10-5-15.	Nil.
1845	Cpl.	Sturrock D.	D.	" " "	10-5-15.	Nil.
275	Sgt.	McAllister	W.	" " "	10-5-15.	Nil.
~~2257~~	"	~~McCleary~~	~~J.~~	" " "		
2536	Cpl.	Ferguson	J.	" " "	10-5-15.	Nil.
1282	"	Callinan	J.	" " "	10-5-15.	Nil.
1766	Pte.	Struthers	W.	" " "	10-5-15.	Nil.
1516	"	Ferguson	C.	" " "	10-5-15.	Nil.
2199	"	Paterson	J.	" " "	10-5-15.	Nil.
1533	"	Jenkinson	J.	" " "	10-5-15.	Nil.
2592	"	Moodie	W.	" " "	10-5-15.	Nil.
1527	L/C.	Lindsay	P.	" " "	10-5-15.	Nil.
2440	"	Thompson	W.	" " "	10-5-15.	Nil.
1469	Pte.	McQueen	M.	REPORTED KILLED	10-5-15.	Nil.
2510	"	Christie	J.	DIED OF WOUNDS.	10-5-15.	Nil.
1072	L/C	Hughes	R.	" " "	10-5-15.	Nil.
1636	Pte.	Hay	A.	GASSED	10-5-15.	Nil.
1349	"	Stewart	J.	"	10-5-15.	Nil.
1218	"	Rankin	T.	"	10-5-15.	Nil.
3193	"	Nicholson	M.	WOUNDED.	10-5-15.	Nil.
2624	"	McCrate	A.	"	10-5-15.	Nil.
2315	"	Conlan	J.	"	10-5-15.	Nil.
2057	"	Higgins	J.	"	10-5-15.	Nil.
2498	"	Brodie	W.	"	10-5-15.	Nil.
1847	"	Paton	J.	"	10-5-15.	Nil.
1460	"	Smith	R.	"	10-5-15.	Nil.
1433	Cpl.	Garrity	T.	"	10-5-15.	Nil.
1921	Pte.	Martin	L.	"	10-5-15.	Nil.
1561	Cpl.	Gibson	R.C.	"	10-5-15.	Nil.
~~2237~~	Pte.	McDermid	R.A. 2614	"	10-5-15.	Nil.
2632	"	O'Rorke	B.	"	10-5-15.	Nil.
2177	"	Weldon	R.	"	12-5-15.	Nil.
478	Cpl.	McDougall	P.	"	8-5-15.	Nil.
1519	Pte.	Boyd	J.	"	8-5-15.	Nil.
2001	"	Mayhew	G.	"	8-5-15.	Nil.
1538	"	Hosie	J.	"	8-5-15.	Nil.
2828	"	Connor	G.	"	10-5-15.	Nil.
1988	"	Lawrence	C.	"	10-5-15.	Nil.
2577	"	Logan	J.	"	10-5-15.	Nil.
2197	"	McDiarmid	L.	"	10-5-15.	Nil.
2580	"	Murray	D.A.	"	10-5-15.	Nil.
731	Sgt.	Sloan	W.	"	10-5-15.	Nil.
1664	Cpl.	Reid	J.	"	10-5-15.	Nil.
1696	"	Bowers	R.	"	10-5-15.	Nil.

CONTINUED. 1/9th. Bn. Argyll & Sutherland Highlanders.

No.	Rank	Surname	Initials	Status	Date	Remarks
2550	Pte.	Hoskins	G.	WOUNDED	10-5-15.	Nil.
2547	"	Hunter	J.	"	10-5-15.	
1846	"	Hay	R.	"	10-5-15.	
1973	"	Hill	A.	"	10-5-15.	
1579	"	Long	J.	"	10-5-15.	
2310	"	McRae	M.	"	10-5-15.	
2629	"	McDougall	W.	"	10-5-15.	
1795	"	McIntyre	J.	"	10-5-15.	
1967	"	McNab	W.	"	10-5-15.	
2097	"	Soutar	C.	"	10-5-15.	
2105	"	Todd	W.	"	10-5-15.	
2113	"	Gallagher	J.	"	10-5-15.	
3203	"	Clelland	W.	"	10-5-15.	
3247	"	Coull	D.	"	10-5-15.	
3103	"	McFadyen	J.	"	8-5-15.	
2249	"	Robertson	J.	"	8-5-15.	
2853	"	Bryce	A.	"	8-5-15.	
2319	"	Taylor	P.	"	8-5-15.	
1079	Sgt.	Stewart	W.M.	"	8-5-15	
2608	Cpl.	McIntyre	J.	"	8-5-15.	
1507	"	Cutland	E.E.	"	8-5-15.	
1765	L/C.	Conbrough	D.	"	8-5-15.	
2093	"	Shanks	R.	"	8-5-15.	
2305	"	Ure	A.	"	8-5-15.	
2375	Pte.	Harrison	W.	"	8-5-15.	
2017	"	Lowrie	W.	"	8-5-15.	
2582	"	Murray	J.H.	"	8-5-15.	
2212	"	McMillan	W.	"	8-5-15.	
1326	"	Scott	J.	"	8-5-15.	
1403	"	Thompson	J.	"	8-5-15.	
1545	Sgt.	Smith	R.C.M.	"	8-5-15.	
1286	L/C.	Young	W.	"	8-5-15.	
2180	"	Gadsby	J.	"	8-5-15.	
1520	"	Forrest	J.	"	8-5-15.	
1885	Pte.	Cantley	G.	"	8-5-15.	
2286	"	Caldwell	W.	"	8-5-15.	
1957	"	Davin	J.	"	8-5-15.	
2284	"	Docherty	W.	"	8-5-15.	
2521	"	Durkin	T.	"	8-5-15.	
2578	"	Lamond	J.G.	"	8-5-15.	
978	Sgt.	Graham	A.	"	8-5-15.	
1717	Pte.	Prior	J.	"	8-5-15.	
571	"	Arnott	T.	"	8-5-15.	
2533	"	Foster	A.	"	8-5-15.	
2013	"	McFall	W.	"	8-5-15.	
1955	"	Gordon	P.	"	8-5-15.	
3199	"	Anderson	T.	"	8-5-15.	
1965	L/C.	Craig	J.	"	8-5-15.	
1664	Cpl.	Reid	J.	"	8-5-15.	
2166	Pte.	Raeside	J.	"	8-5-15.	
1468	"	Riddell	J.	"	8-5-15.	
2165	"	Robb	J.	"	8-5-15.	
2135	L/C.	Kirks	S.	"	8-5-15.	
2639	Pte.	Procter	J.	"	8-5-15.	
1833	"	Murray	A.	"	8-5-15.	
298	L/C.	Hughes	R.			
298	L/C.	McCallum		"	9-5-15.	
2984	Pte.	Irvine	D.	"	9-5-15.	
2120	"	Adams	J.	"	9-5-15.	
2551	"	Howie	F.	"	9-5-15.	
3116	"	Campbell	J.	"	9-5-15.	
1725	"	Gillies	J.	"	9-5-15.	
2127	"	Blair	M.	"	9-5-15.	
2652	Sgt.	Smith	W.M.	"	9-5-15.	
2508	Cpl.	Thompson	R.	"	9-5-15.	
1404	L/C.	McGillveray	J.	"	9-5-15.	

Reported by O.C. Unit

CONTINUED.   1/9th. Argyll & Sutherland Highlanders.

2251	Pte.	Blythe	J.	WOUNDED.	9-5-15.
2489	"	Brooks	J.	"	9-5-15.
2485	"	Anderson	J.	"	9-5-15
3034	"	Clyde	R.	"	9-5-15.
1942	"	Divers	J.	"	9-5-15.
2524	"	Drummond	G.	"	9-5-15.
1634	"	McInnes	G.A.	"	9-5-15.
3141	"	Murray	J.	"	9-5-15.
2829	"	Whyte	N.	"	9-5-15.
53	L/C.	Boyle	N.	"	9-5-15.
2182	Pte.	McMillan	W.	"	10-5-15.
1863	"	Glen	N.	"	10-5-15.
1896	"	Cunningham	T.	"	10-5-15.
2181	"	Hamilton	A.	"	10-5-15.
1641	"	Hunter	D.	"	10-5-15.
2006	"	Guthrie	J.	"	10-5-15.
2905	"	Elspie	A.	"	10-5-15.
1401	L/C.	Hamilton	J.	"	10-5-15.
1961	Pte.	Kerr	J.	"	10-5-15.
2296	"	McDiarmid	J.	"	10-5-15.
1884	"	Craig	J.	"	10-5-15.
2140	"	McIntyre	H.	"	10-5-15.
1532	"	Malcolm	T.	"	10-5-15.
1883	"	Hemmill	R.	"	10-5-15.
2185	"	Cullin	J.	"	10-5-15.
2199	"	James	W.	"	10-5-15.
2448	"	Brodie	J.G.	"	10-5-15.
864	Sgt.	Swan	T.	"	10-5-15.
991	"	Brown	H.B.	"	10-5-15.
1704	Pte.	Nisbet	J.	"	10-5-15.
2519	"	Connolly	M.	"	10-5-15.
2044	"	Gilchrist	D.	"	10-5-15.
1703	"	McWilliam	J.	"	10-5-15.
2964	L/C.	Gartshore	J.	"	10-5-15.
1622	Pte.	Munro	R.	"	10-5-15.
2753	"	Wilson	J.	"	10-5-15.
2505	Cpl.	Blair	J.C.	"	10-5-15.
2517	Pte.	Cowden	J.	"	10-5-15.
2525	"	Donaldson	R.	"	10-5-15.
2665	"	Taylor	R.	"	10-5-15.
1849	L/C.	Carson	J.C.	"	10-5-15.
2502	Pte.	Bald	J.M.	"	10-5-15.
2252	"	Crane	W.	"	10-5-15.
2635	"	Potter	S.	"	10-5-15.
2667	"	Thomson	J.S.	"	10-5-15.
2688	"	Allan	G.M.	"	10-5-15.
2847	L/C	Pollock	S.	"	10-5-15.
2983	"	Fraser	J.	"	10-5-15.
682	Sgt.	Wilson	W.	"	10-5-15.
1103	Cpl.	Campbell	J.F.	"	10-5-15.
2322	L/C.	Coutts	W.L.	"	10-5-15.
2053	Pte.	Clylle	J.	"	10-5-15.
2476	"	Duffy	T.	"	10-5-15.
2562	L/C.	Hartley	D.	"	10-5-15.
1250	Pte.	Laidlaw	W.	"	10-5-15.
1707	"	McDougall	J.	"	10-5-15.
1706	"	Sharkey	N.	"	10-5-15.
2359	"	Barnes	R.	"	10-5-15.
2343	"	Campbell	T.	"	10-5-15.
2522	"	Dickson	J.	"	10-5-15.
2027	"	Lees	W.	"	10-5-15.
2161	Cpl.	McDermott	J.	"	10-5-15.
2414	Pte.	Thomson	W.	"	10-5-15.
2257	Sgt.	McCleary	J.	"	10-5-15.

Casualties.   No? I District.

1/9th. Bn. Argyll & Sutherland Highlanders.

Regl No.	Rank & Name	Casualty		Prev. Rpd. Casualty.
2091	Pte. McMillan G.	WOUNDED IN ACTION	10/5/15.	Nil.
2561	Pte. Hay J.	do.	10/5/15.	Nil.
1077	Sgt. Tavendale T.A.	do.	do.	Nil.
2007	Sgt. Lees A.	do.	do.	Nil.
2188	Pte. Blyth W.	do.	8/5/15.	Nil.
1858	Pte. Chalmers A.	do.	8/5/15.	Nil.
2227	Pte. Clyde W.	do.	do.	Nil.
2364	Pte. Christie P.	do.	do.	Nil.
2279	Pte. Mathie (Mathie G.	do.	11/5/15.	Nil.
1430	Cpl. Sutherland J.	do.	10/5/15.	Nil.
1918	Pte. Nairn W.	do.	do.	Nil.
2274	L.Cpl. Martin J?	do.	do.	Nil.
2035	Pte. Gillespie J.	do.	11/5/15.	Nil.
2316	Pte. Martin J.	do.	do.	Nil.
2265	Pte. McArthur J.	do.	do.	Nil.
1748	L.Cpl. Morrison C.D.	do.	do.	Nil.
832	L.Cpl. Morrison J.E.	do.	10/do.	Nil.
2587	Pte. Allan W.G.	do.	11/5/15.	Nil.
1764	Pte. Lament F.	do.	10/5/15.	Nil.
2224	Cpl. Gray T.	do.	do.	Nil.
2586	Pte. Mair D.	do.	do.	Nil.
1594	Pte. Gray T.	do.	do.	Nil.
1768	Pte. Nugent R.	do.	do.	Nil.
1881	Sgt. Gilchrist A.	do.	do.	Nil.
2559	Pte. Umpherson A.	do.	do.	Nil.
3231	Pte. Sloan J.	do.	do.	Nil.
2297	Pte. McLean D.	do.	do.	Nil.
1818	Pte. Tiernan F.	do.	do.	Nil.
2527	Pte. Elliot N.	do.	do.	Nil.

The above reported by O.C. The Battalion 14/5/15.

| 1736 | Cpl. Bell R. | DIED FROM WOUNDS RECEIVED IN ACTION | 13/5/15. | Nil. |

The above reported by O.C. No. 8 C.C. SStation. 20/5/15.

Capt. For.
O. I/c. Terr. Infantry Records, 3rd. Echelon.
G.H.Q. 21/5/15.

Casualties.   No. I District.
                I/9th. Bn. The Argyll & Sutherland Highlanders.

Regl. No.	Rank & Name	Casualty	Prev. Rpd. Casualty.
	LIEUT. ANDERSON	A.D.M. KILLED IN ACTION 8/5/15.	NIL%
	LIEUT. NAPIER	H.A.M. WOUNDED IN ACTION 8/5/15.	NIL.

Reported by O. C. The Battalion 14/5/15.

                                        HB   Capt. for.
                O. I/c. Terr. Infantry Records, 3rd. Echelon,
                        G.H.Q.   21/5/15.

CASUALTIES MAY 22nd. 1915 No 1 DISTRICT.

9th. ARGYLE & SUTHERLAND HIGHLANDERS.

Regt. No.	Rank & Name	CASUALTY		Previously Reptd.
1973	Pte Hill A.	DIED OF WOUNDS G.S.W.Thigh & Side.11/5/15. Reported by No. 8 Cas. Clrg Stn.12/5/15.		Nil.
2498	Pte Brodie W.	DIED OF WOUNDS G.S.W.Leg.12/5/15 Reported by No. 2 Cas.Clrg.Hospital 12/5/15.		Nil.
2089	Lce Cpl Halsey R.	Discharged To Duty.14/5/15. Rptd By Con Dept. Rouen 14/5/15.		Sick.
1594	Pte Gray C.	ditto	ditto ditto	Sick.
1686	Pte Boyd D.	ditto	ditto ditto	Wounded
2578	Pte Lamont J.	ditto	ditto ditto	Wounded
2319	Pte Taylor P.	ditto	ditto ditto	Sick
2124	Lce Cpl Hislop D.	G.S.W.Shldr.Admitted No1.Canadian Field Ambulance 27/4/15.Reptd By O.C.Fld Amb.2/5/15.		Nil.
226	Pte Johnston E.	Discharged To Duty 10/5/15 Reported by O.C. Con Dept Rouen 10/5/15.		Sick.
1869	Pte Bryan P.	S.Wound Head.Admitted 81st.Field Amb 6/5/15. Reptd. by O.C.Field Amb.8/5/15.		Nil.
2637	Pte Pollock J.	DIARRHOEA.Admitted 81st. Field Amb. 6/5/15 Reported by O.C.Field Amb.8/5/15.		Nil.
2167	Pte Kennedy T.	Discharged To Duty 27/4/15. Reported by O.C. Con Dept.Rouen 27/4/15.		Wounded.
2572	Pte Kennedy T.	ditto	10/5/15. 10/5/15.	do.
1551	Pte Clacherty M.	ditto	10/5/15 10/5/15	do.
408	C.S.M.Sneddon W.	ditto	16/5/15. 16/5/15.	Sick.
3181	Pte Elsby R.	ditto	16/5/15. 16/5/15.	Sick.
2998	Pte Anderson J.	ditto	16/5/15. 16/5/15.	Sick.
2667	Pte Thomson J.	ditto	16/5/15. 16/5/15.	Wounded.
2079	Pte Machie G.	ditto	17/5/15. 17/5/15.	do.
2307	Pte McLaren S.	ditto	17/5/15. 17/5/15	do.
2507	Cpl Cutland E.	ditto	17/5/15. 17/5/15	do.
1756	Pte Campbell D.	ditto	13/5/15. 13/5/15.	Sick.
2569	Pte Kyle J.	ditto	30/4/15. 83rd Field Amb 2/5/15.	Sick.
1984	Pte Neil C.	B.Wd Head.Admttd 81st Field Amb.25/4/15 Reptd By O.C.Field Amb.1/5/15.		Nil
2569	Pte Kyle J.	Sick.admittd 27/4/15.ditto 1/5/15.		Nil.
2135	Lce Cpl Kirk S.	Wounded 8/5/15.Reptd By O.C.Unit14/5/15.		Nil.
2237	Pte Brown A.	Wounded 10/5/15. ditto ditto		Nil.
2267	Pte McGeachy F.	VARICOCELE admttd 4/5/15.Reptd by 83rd Fld Amb.9/5/15.		NIL.
631	Pte Kilpatrick	INFLUENZA. do. 2/5/15. ditto.		NIL.
1396 Pt	Pte McKirdy A.	SPRD.ANKLE do. 3/5/15. ditto.		Nil.
2309	Pte O'Brian P.	S.Wd HEAD Tonsilitis 7/5/15. ditto.		NIL.
259	Sgt.Grant G.	RHEUMATISM. admttd 8/5/15. ditto.		NIL.
2290	Pte Urquhart J.	INDIGESTION do 8/5/15. ditto.		NIL.
1816	Pte Hannah H.	Nervous Debility 8/5/15. ditto.		NIL.
2302	Pte Begg A.	Nervous Debility 8/5/15. ditto.		NIL.
2282	Pte Bennie P.	Varicose Veins 8/5/15. ditto.		NIL.
2647	Pte Rafferty J.	RHEUMATISM. 5/5/15 Dischgd To Duty 9/5/15. ditto.		NIL.

For O.R.Sgt.

9th. Argyle & Sutherland Highlanders.

CASUALTIES.   NO. 1 DISTRICT.

1/9th Bn. Argyll & Sutherland Highlanders T.F.

Regtl.No.	Rank & Name.		Casualty.	By whom reported.	P.R.
2688	Pte. Allan	G.	DIED OF WOUNDS. 13/5/15.	O.C., No.3 Cas. Cl.Stn. 16/5/15.	W.
731	Sgt. Sloan	W.	To England per H.S.Anglia.13/5/15.	H.Ship thro' D.A.Q.MG. Boulogne.13/5/15.	W.
1795	Pte. Macintyre	J.	do.	do.	W.
2984	Pte. Irvine	D.	do.	do.	W.
2260	L/Sgt. Herd	M.	do.	do.	W.
2436	Pte. Hunter	A.	do.	do.	W.
1703	Pte. MacWilliams	J.	do.	do.	W.
2017	Pte. Lowry	W.	To Englnad per H.S.Anglia 11/5/15.	H.Ship. 11/5/15.	W.
2057	Pte. Higgins	J.	do. 12/5/15.	do.12/5/15.	W.
682	Sgt. Wilson	W.	do. 13/5/15.	do.13/5/15.	W.
2064	Pte. Young	R.	To England per H.S. St.Petersburg. 19/5/15.	O.C., Re-inforcements Rouen.19/5.	W.
2167	Pte. Kennedy	T.	do.	do.	W.
1817	Pte. Macbride	D.	do.	do.	W.
778	L/C. Borland	W.	do.	do.	W.
2315	Pte. Coulon	J.	To England per H.S St.Patrick.13/5/15.	D.A.Q.M.G. Boulogne 13/5/15.	W.
2030	Pte. Lowry	A.	do.	do.	W.
2305	L/C. Mure	A.	do.	do.	W.
2237	Pte. Brown	A.	To Englnad per H.S.Brighton 13/5/15.	do.	W.
2485	Pte. Anderson	J.	To England per H.S. Anglia. 14/5/15.	O.C.,H.Ship.	W.
1218	Pte. Rankine	T.	To England per H.S. Brighton 13/5/15.	D.A.Q.M.G.13/5.	W.
2556	Pte. Hall	A.	To England per H.S. St.Andrew.12/5/15.	O.C.,H.Ship.	W.
2033	Pte. Gillespie	J.D.	To England per H.S. Valdivia. 13/5/15.	do.	W.
1816	Pte. Hannah	H.	do.	do.	W.
1706	Pte. Sharkey	N.	do.	do.	W.

2. 9/Argylls.

	Captain ERSKINE ✗ J.A.E.	To England per H.S.Atalanta.15/5/15.	O.C. Re-inforcements.Rouen. 15/5/15.	N.
1848	Pte. Thompson W.	To England per H.S. Brighton 8/5/15.	D.A.Q.M.G. Boulogne.8/5.	W.
1809	Pte. Muir W.	To duty at Terr.I. Base."A" Rouen.19/5/15.	O.C.,Con. Depot.19/5.	N.
2853	Pte. Bryce A.	do.	do.	W.

✗ Not being in the nature of a Casualty, this has not been reported to War Office

J Gladwell Cpl a/s

General Headquarters, 3rd Echelon. 24/5/15.

L/Cpl. John Hood for ORSgt.

CASUALTIES&.   No.1 DISTRICT.

1/9th Bn. Argyll & Sutherland Highrs.

Regtl.No.	Rank & Name.	Casualty.	By whom reported.	P.R.
2561 2526	Pte. Hay, J.	To England, 13/5/15. Reported by O/C Hospl.Ship "St.Andrew"		Wounded.
2519	Pte. Connolly, M.	do.		do.
2612	Pte. McDonald, H.	do.		do.
2953	Pte. Robertson, J.	do.		NIL.
823	L/C. Morrison, J.E.	do.		Wounded.
478	Pte. McDougall, P.	To England, 10/5/15. Reported O/C Hospl.Ship "Brighton".		do.
2234	Pte. Docherty, W.	do.		do.
1576	Pte. Davidson, G.	To duty: 22/5/15. O/C Con.Dpt,Rouen.		do.

....

L/C John d Hood   For Orderly Room Sergeant,
                   1/9th Bn, Argyllshire & Sutherlandshire Highlanders.

G.H.Q.,
3rd Echelon,
25/5/15.

1/9th. Bn. The Ar[gyll] & Sutherland Highdrs.

CASUALTIES.   No.1. DISTRICT.

Regt.No.	Rank & Name.		Casualty.	P.R.
2309	Pte. O'Brien	J.	Died from Gas Poisoning. 25/5/15. (Report by O/C. No.12. Fld. Ambce. 25/5/15)	N.
1634	. McInnes	G.A.	To Duty with Bn. 12/5/15. (Report by O/C. Bn. 14/5/15.)	W.
3502	. Bald	J.	------ do. ------ 13/5/15.	W.
2252	. Crane	W.	------ do. ------ 13/5/15.	W.
2562	. Hartley	D.	------ do. ------ 13/5/15.	W.
1532	. Malcolm	T.	------ do. ------ 13/5/15.	W.
2188	. Blyth	W.	------ do. ------ 13/5/15.	W.
1349	. Stewart	J.	------ do. ------ 13/5/15.	W.
2546	. Guthrie	W.	To Duty at Rouen. 21/4/15. (Report by O/C. Con. Depot. Rouen. 21/4/15.)	W.
1693	. Simpson	R.	To Duty at Rouen. 16/5/15. (Report by O/C. Con. Depot. Rouen. 16/5/15.)	S.
2539	. Gillies	W.	To Duty at Rouen. 25/5/15. (Report by O/C. Con. Depot. Rouen. 25/5/15.)	W.
257	C.S.M. Diamond	J.	To Duty at Rouen. 18/5/15. (Report by O/C. Con. Depot. Rouen. 18/5/15.)	S.
2025	Pte. Stoddart	A.	To Duty at Rouen. 21/5/15. (Report by O/C. Con. Depot. Rouen. 21/5/15.)	W.
2667	. Thomson	J.S.	To Duty at Rouen. 16/5/15. (Report by O/C. Con. Depot. Rouen. 16/5/15.)	W.
2964	L/C. Gatshore	J.	To Duty at Rouen. 20/5/15. (Report by O/C. Con. Depot. Rouen. 20/5/15.)	W.
1394	Pte. Cullen	N.	N.Y.D. Ad. 82nd. F.A. 11/5/15. Discharged to Duty. 13/5/15. (Report by O/C. 82nd. F.A. 14/5/15.)	N.

G.H.Q. 3rd. Echelon.
    31/5/15.

10th Inf.Bde.
4th Div.

7th & 9th BATTNS. THE ARGYLL & SUTHERLAND HIGHLANDERS.
(Composite Battalion)

J U N E

1 9 1 5

(Note: The 7th & 9th Battns. The Argyll & Sutherland Highlanders were organized as a Composite Battalion on 27.5.15. Independent formations were resumed on 21.7.15, the 9th Battn. being transferred to VI. Corps as Corps Troops).

Attached:

Casualty Lists.

Army Form C. 2118.

Ref. map - Sheet "B" Ypres

WAR DIARY
or
INTELLIGENCE SUMMARY
(Erase heading not required.)

Composite Battn. A & S. Highlrs

1915

Instructions regarding War Diaries and Intelligence Summaries are contained in F. S. Regs., Part II. and the Staff Manual respectively. Title pages will be prepared in manuscript.

Hour, Date, Place	Summary of Events and Information	Remarks and References to Appendices
June		
1st 9. a.m.	Battn. left billets at Farms A.16 Rested at wood B.3.c. and proceeded at 8 p.m. to Canal bank B.15.c. to dugouts. Provided carrying and working parties for R.E. and battns in firing line	
2nd to 5th June	do — do —	
5th June 3 p.m.	Proceeded to bivouacs at Chateau. B.3.c. bivouacs.	
5th to 7th June		
7th June 7.30 p.m.	Proceeded to dugouts and farms in B.17.c. in reserve for 16th Inf. Brigade.	
8th to 11th June	Provided carrying and working parties for R.E. and battns in firing line	
11th June 10 p.m.	Battn. proceeded to Billets at A.21.a.b.	
12th to 16th June	in billets.	
16th June 7.30 p.m.	Proceeded to dugouts at B.17.	
17th to 22nd June	Provided carrying and working parties for R.E. and battns in firing line including specialists work, mining, driving wells and in trenches.	
22nd June	During the night 21/22 June 8 men wounded (7 from shell fire.)	
26th June	Draft of 6 Officers (3 from 2/7 Argylls 3 from 2/9 Argylls) arrived in front line —	
23/30th June	Provided carrying & working parties for R.G. and battns on 29th June. One man killed on 29th June.	

CASUALTY LISTS.

1/9th.Batt.Argylle & Sutherland Highlanders.

Casualties.   No 1 District.

Regt.No	Rank & Name.	Casualty.	P.R.
	CAPTAIN BAIRD F.M.	GASSED 24/5/15. Reported by O.C. 27/5/15. Bn.	Nil.
	CAPTAIN BROWN A.G.	MISSING REPORTED WOUNDED. 24/5/15. Reported by O.C. 27/5/15. Bn.	Nil.
	LIEUT. OWEN O.A.	MISSING. 24/5/15. Reported by O.C.Bn. 27/5/15.	Nil.
	LIEUT. CHRYSTAL G.G.	MISSING. 24/5/15. Reported by O.C.Bn. 27/5/15.	Nil.
	CAPTAIN FINDLAY R.S. *	KILLED IN RAILWAY DISASTER AT CARLISLE 23/5/15. Reported by O.C.Bn. 27/5/15-	Nil.
	LIEUT. BONNAR J.C. *	do Do	Nil.
	LIEUT. KIRSOP P.A. *	SERIOUSLY INJURED IN RAILWAY DISASTER 23/5/15. Reported by O.C.Bn. 27/5/15.	Nil,
	LIEUT. JACKSON J. *	KILLED IN RAILWAY DISASTER. 23/5/15- Reported by O.C.BN. 27/5/15.	S.

* These Officers were proceeding home on Leave.

G.H.Q. 3rd.Echelon.
1/6/15.

116

TWO
3/6

1/9th Battn, Argylle & Sutherland Hdrs.

Casualties.   No 1 District.

Regt. No.	Rank & Name	Casualty.	P.R.
No 1916	Pte. Davidson R.	Killed in Action 24/5/15. Reported by O.C.Batt. 28/5/15.	Nil.
1140	Srgt. Fulton J.	do.	do.
1938	Pte. Dollan W.	do.	do.
2513	Cpl. Chalmers J.	do.	do.
2502	Pte. Bauld J.M.	Wounded in Action 24/5/15. Reported by O.C.Battn.28/5/15.	Nil.
1634	: McInnes G.A.	do.	do.
1944	: Gray A.	do.	do.
3081	: Connacher D.	do.	do.
3208	Cpl. Greenwood T.	do.	do.
3010	L/Cpl Anderson W.	do.	do.
1916	Sgt. Taylor J.	do.	do.
1590	Cpl. Harrison G.	do.	do.
2516	: Campbell A.G.	do.	do.
2601	Pte. McNiven D.	do.	do.
2583	: Monaghan D.	do.	do.
2858	: Sinclair J.	do.	do.
2084	: Anderson J.	do.	do.
2755	: Brennan J.	do.	do.
2278	: Graham A.	do.	do.
2156	: McKenzie J.	do.	do.
1735	: Sherwood G.	do.	do.
2412	: Todd D.	do.	do.
2860	: Larmont J.	do.	do.
3172	: Ure A.	do.	do.
1976	: Coyle M.	do.	do.
2595	: McLoughlan P.	do.	do.
1493	: Phillips C.	do.	do.
2689	: Anderson R.	do.	do.
3071	L/Cpl McTee R.	do.	do.
1841	Pte. Begg J.	do.	do.
3019	: Gemmell J.	do.	do.
1288	Cpl. Hay J.	do.	do.
2012	Pte. Carmichael A.	do.	do.
1399	: Halkett T.	do.	do.
936	Sgt. Duncan G.	do.	do.
1842	Pte. Bonnar J.	do.	do.
2495	: Burr J.	do.	do.
2014	: Neil A.	do.	do.
1595	: Melvin J.	do.	do.
3101	: Leishman A.	do.	do.
2325	: Boyce C.	Gassed in Action 24/5/15- Reported by O.C.Batt.28/5/15	do.
1407	: Brown J.S.	do.	do.
2486	Cpl. Bryden W.M.	do.	do.
2504	Pte. Burnett J.	do.	do.
1850	: Dempster W.	do.	do.
2526	: Donaldson R.	do.	do.
2712	: Gillies R.	do.	do.
2250	: McRae A.	do.	do.
1635	: Muir W.	do.	do.
314	L/Cpl Dale R.	do.	do.
1411	: Lyle D.	do.	do.
1498	Pte. Anderson T.	do.	do.
1558	: Blue W.	do.	do.
1928	: Cranston R.	do.	do.

1/9th Battn. Argyll & Sutherland Hdrs.

Casualties continued.

Regt. Nos	Rank & Name	Casualty	P.R.
No 2528	Pte. Erskine J.	Gassed in Action 24/5/15. Reported by O.C.Batt. 28/5/15.	Nil.
No 2576	" Lilburn S.	do.	do.
" 1930	" Logan J.	do.	do.
" 1432	" McPherson T.	do.	do.
" 1688	" McVey J.	do.	do.
" 1698	" Stevenson J.	do.	do.
" 1569	" Swanson G.	do.	do.
" 2684	" Watson A.	do.	do.
" 1983	" Cochrane J.	do.	do.
" 1972	" Duncan A.	do.	do.
" 2562	" Hartley D.	do.	do.
" 2072	" Paxton W.	do.	do.
" 2459	" McKenzie R.	do.	do.
" 2475	" Murphy W.	do.	do.
" 2360	" Byrne T.	do.	do.
" 1699	Cpl. McIntyre S.	do.	do.
" 2626	Pte. McIntyre D.	do.	do.
" 2210	" McKinlay G.	do.	do.
" 2991	" Stevens T.	do.	do.
" 3219	" McWilliams D.	do.	do.
" 75	A/Reg.S.M. Hosie J.	do.	do.
" 1880	L/Cpl. Coubrough E.	do.	do.
" 2184	" Crawford A.	do.	do.
" 2036	Drummer Bell W.	do.	do.
" 2067	Pte. Charity J.	do.	do.
" 1677	" Haggerty G.	do.	do.
" 1877	" Mitchell R.	do.	do.
" 2335	" O'Hare J.	do.	do.
" 1449	" Paul L.	do.	do.
" 657	Sgt. Sinclair D.B.	do.	do.
" 477	L/Sgt. Logan G.	do.	do.
" 1815	Pte. Baird J.	do.	do.
" 2904	" Brady J.	do.	do.
" 1448	" Clark J.	do.	do.
" 1909	" McDonald M.	do.	do.
" 1339	" McEwan A.	do.	do.
" 2196	" Hamilton G.	do.	do.
" 2680	" Whyte A.P.	do.	do.
" 2839	" Campbell J.	do.	do.
" 3105	" McIntyre J.	do.	do.
" 3169	" Nugent R.	do.	do.
" 2877	" Louden J. (Louden)	do.	do.
" 3007	" Wilson G.	do.	do.
" 726	" Meek J.F.	do.	do.
" 2133	" Johnstone R.	do.	do.
" 2010	" Kelly J.	do.	do.
" 1695	" Lindsay J.	do.	do.
" 1851	" McLean H.	do.	do.
" 1838	" McQuat T.	do.	do.
1717	" Sheridan J. ((also believed to be wounded))	do.	do.
" 2681	" Wilson D.	Gassed in action	do.
" 861	Cpl. Inch R.	do.	do.
" 2560	Pte. Handyside R.	do.	do.
" 2616	" McTaggart S.	do.	do.
" 1740	" Smith W.	do.	do.
" 2411	Cpl. Smith M.	do.	do.

xxx2520xxxxRte.xxxConleyxxxxxJ.xxxxMissingx(reportedxwoundedx).

2/6/15

Captain
for Officer i/c Territorial Infantry Records
G.H.Q. 3rd. Echelon.

1/9th. Argyll & Sutherland Hdrs.

Casualties. No I District.

Regtl. No.	Rank & Name	Casualty	P.R.
2418	Pte. Walker D.	Died of Wounds 31/5/15 Reported by O.C. No 8 C.C.Stn. 31/5/15.	Nil.
2803	Pte. Black J.	Missing (believed to be killed) reported by O.C. Batt. 28/5/15.	Nil.
786	C.Q.M.S. Thomson J.	To duty 26/5/15 at Rouen Reported by O.C.Con Depot 26/5/15.	Nil.
2276	Pte. Penney D.	To duty 28/5/15 at Rouen Reported by O.C.Con.Depot 28/5/15.	W.
1770	Pte. Jarvie W.	To Duty 21/5/15 at Rouen. Reported by O.C.Con.Depot 21/5/15	S.
2465	Pte. McClary J.	To Duty 27/5/15 at Rouen Reported by O.C.Con Depot 27/5/15.	W.
2198	Pte. Niven J.	To Duty 29/5/15 at Rouen. Reported by O.C. Con Depot 29/5/15	Nil.
1664	Cpl. Reid J.	To Duty 29/5/15 at Rouen Reported by O.C. Con Depot 29/5/15	W.
1180	Pte. McMurray, A.	To Duty 29/5/15 at Rouen Reported by O.C.Con Depot 29/5/15	S.
1738	Pte. Ness A.	To Duty at Rouen 29/5/15 Reported by O.C.Conv Depot 29/5/15	S.
2184	L/Cpl Crawford A.	To Duty at Rouen 29/5/15 Reported by O.C.Conv Depot. 29/5/15	Nil.
2161	L/Cpl. McDermott J.	To Duty at Rouen 18/5/15 Reported by O.C.Conv Depot 18/5/15	W.
1781	Pte. Bissett W.	To Duty Base Detail Boulogne 15/5/15 Reported by O.C. Base details Boulogne 15/5/15	W.
3037	Pte. Dodds W.	To Duty at Rouen 30/5/15 Reported by O.C.Conv Depot 30/5/15	Nil.
2596	Pte. McGirr G.	To Duty at Rouen 30/5/15 Reported by O.C.Conv Depot 30/5/15	S.
2007	Sgt. Lees A.	To Duty at Rouen 30/5/15 Reported by O.C.Conv Depot 30/5/15	W.
2528	Pte. Erskine S.	To Duty at Rouen 30/5/15 Reported by O.C.Conv Depot 30/5/15	G.
2482	Pte. Allan G.	To Duty at Rouen 30/5/15 Reported by O.C.Conv Depot 30/5/15	Nil.
477	Sgt. Logan G.	To Duty at Rouen 30/5/15 Reported by O.C.Conv Depot 30/5/15	Nil.

1/ h Batt. Argyll & Sutherland Hdrs.

Casualties Contd.   No1 District.

Regtl. No.	Rank & Name	Casualty	P.R.
No 1635	Pte. Muir W.	To Duty 30/5/15 at Rouen Reported by O.C.Conv.Depot 31/5/15	Nil.
2626	Pte. McIntyre D.	To Duty at Rouen 31/5/15 Reported by O.C.Conv Depot 31/5/15	Nil.
314	L/Cpl Dale R.	To Duty at Rouen 31/5/15 Reported by O.C.Conv Depot 31/5/15	Nil.
2569	Pte. Kyle J.	To Duty at Rouen 31/5/15 Reported by O.C.Conv Depot 31/5/15	Nil.
2616	Pte. McTaggart S.	To Duty at Rouen 30/5/15 Reported by O.C.Conv Depot 30/5/15	Nil.

4TH.June 1915.

                   Captain
         for Officer i/c Terr.Inf. Records
           G.H.Q.   3/Echelon.

CASUALTIES   No. 1. District.

1/9th. Bn. ARGYLL and SUTHERLAND HIGHLANDERS

Regtl. No. Rank and Name	Casualty	Reptd. by	Prevs reptd.
2nd.LIEUT.R.G.SELLARS.	G.S.W.LEFT FOREARM 6/6/15.	Reptd. by A.D.M.S. 51st.Highrs Division	Nil.
2480.Pte. Aitken A.	To England 26/5/15.	M.L.O. Boulogne.	W'dd.
1902.Pte. Lambert J.	Admitted Hospl.26/5/15. Sick.	O.C.172.Coy. Royal Engr.	Nil.
2426.Pte. Robertson J.	Discharged Hosp. to Duty 25/5/15.	O.C.172 Coy. Royal Engrs.	Nil.
2365.Pte. Christie. W.	Admitted 10 Field Ambce. 10/5/15. G.S.W.Ear.	O.C,10 Field Ambulance.	Nil.
2052.Pte. Dorward. D.	MISSING 11/5/15.	O.C.Unit.	Nil.
2648.Pte. Ritchie. J.	-----ditto-----	-- do --	Nil.
2264.Pte. McBryde. J.	---- ditto ----	-- do --	Nil.
2607.Pte. McKinlay J.	---- ditto ----	-- do --	Nil.
2327.Pte. Ferguson A.	To England 26/5/15.	Under Auth. D.A.G.L.d- 25/5/15.	Nil.
2126.Pte. Young J.	To England 26/5/15.	-- ditto --	Nil.
1551.Pte. Clacherty M.	----- ditto -----	-- ditto --	Nil.
169.Pte. Wilson A.	----- ditto -----	-- ditto---	Nil.
3010.L/C. Anderson W.	To England 26/5/15.	M.L.O.,D.A.Q.M.G. Boulogne.	W'dd.
2520.Pte. Conley James.	To England 27/5/15. (G.S.W.Elbow)	O.C.Hosp.Ship (Name not known)	W'dd.

10/6/15.

CASUALTIES.

No.1 District
1/9th Bn. Argyll & Sutherland Highrs.

Regtl.No.	Rank & Name.	Casualty.	Reptd By	P.R.
2181.	Pte Hamilton A.	To England 13/5/15.	O.C.Hosp.Ship St Andrew 13/5/15	W.
2537.	PTE Gillies A.	To England 27/5/15,	O.C.Hosp.Ship St Andrew 27/5/15.	S.
2639.	Pte. Proctor J.	To England 11/5/15.	O.C.Hosp.Ship H.S.Salta 11/5/15.	W.
2551	Pte Howie F.	To England 11/5/15-	O.C.HospShip H.S.Salta 11/5/15.	W.
1797	Pte Prior J.	To England 11/5/15.	O.C.Hosp.Ship H.S.Salta 11/5/15-	W.
1900	Pte Anderson W.	To England 17/5/15.	O.C.Hosp.Ship Anglia. 17/5/15.	W
1728	Pte. Mc Nicol S.	Missing. 24/5/15.	Reported by O.C.Bn.26/5/15-	N.
2678	Pte. Wheldon. D.	Ditto. Ditto.	Ditto.	N.
2024.	BEb. Arthur. J. Atkin.	Ditto. Ditto.	Ditto.	N.
1804.	Pte. Atkin. J.	Ditto. Ditto.	Ditto.	N.
1737.	Pte. Creelmen.W.	Ditto. Ditto.	Ditto.	N.
2673.	Pte. Thomson J.	Ditto. Ditto.	Ditto.	N.
1652.	Pte. West. F.	Ditto. Ditto.	Ditto.	N.
2416.	Pte. Wilson H.	Ditto. Ditto.	Ditto.	N.
2915.	Pte. Lennen. Hz	Ditto. Ditto.	Ditto.	N.
3268.	Pte. Nugent. G.	Ditto. Ditto.	Ditto.	N.
2975.	Pte. Nugent. J.	Ditto. Ditto.	Ditto.	N.
2277.	Pte.Taylor. J.	Ditto. Ditto.	Ditto.	N.
1632.	Pte. Malarvie J.	Ditto. Ditto.	Ditto.	N.
1479.	Pte. Millar T.	Ditto. Ditto.	Ditto.	N.
1593.	Pte. Crearer J.	Ditto. Ditto.	Ditto.	N.
2204.	Cpl. Robertson P.	Missing (reported wounded) 24/5/15.	Ditto.	N.
1913.	Pte. Lee. W.	Missing 24/5/15.	Ditto.	N
2077.	Pte. Semple F.	Ditto. Ditto.	Ditto.	N.
1864.	Pte. Coyne T.	Ditto. Ditto.	Ditto.	N.
1743.	Pte. Cowan. A.	Ditto. Ditto.	Ditto.	N.
1970.	Ptr. Docherty. M.	Ditto. Ditto.(reported wounded)	Ditto.	N.

Casualties (continued) Sheet E.

Rrgtl. No.	Rank and Name	Casualty.		By whom reported	Prevs reptd.
2651.	Pte. Sleeth. E.	Missing	24/5/15.	Reported by O.C. Bn. 28/5/15.	N.
2558.	Pte. Hamill. J.	Ditto.	Ditto.	Ditto.	N.

17/6/15.

CASUALTIES   No.1.DISTRICT

1/9th. Bn. ARGYLL & SUTHERLAND HIGHLANDERS

Regtl. No.	Rank and Name	Casualty	By Whom reported	Prevs. reptd.
2287.	Pte. Lowe. H.	DIED OF WOUNDS 27/5/15.	O&C.3.Cas. Clear.Statn.	Nil.
2135.	L/C. Kirk. S.	DIED OF WOUNDS 9/5/15.	O.C.82nd.Fd. Ambulance.	W'dd.
2246.	Pte. Craig.T.	Transferred to England 9/6/15.	O.C.H/S.St. Andrew.	W'dd.
1519.	Pte. Boyd. J.	Transferred to England, 17/5/15.	O.C.H/S. St.Patrick.	W'dd.
861.	Cpl. Inch. R.	Transferred to England. 9/6/15.	O.C.H/S. St. Patrick.	W'dd.

23/6/15.

CASUALTIES   No.1. DISTRICT

1/9th.Bn.ARGYLL & SUTHER. HIGHLANDERS

Regtl. No.	Rank and Name	Casualty	By whom reported.	Prevs. reptd.
2332.	L/C Dennaett T.	GASSED. 25/5/15.	O.C. 10 Fd. Ambce.	Nil.
2732.	Pte.McPherson. J.	---- Ditto ----	-- ditto--	Nil.
1864.	Pte. Coyne T.	GASSED 25/5/15.	-- ditto--	Missing. (24/5/15)
2179.	Pte. McGawan. J.	----- Ditto ----	---ditto---	Nil.
2875.	Pte. Wallace. J.	----- Ditto ----	--- ditto---	Nil.
2471.	Pte. Brown W.	----- Ditto-----	---- ditto ---	Nil.
2259.	L/C. Forrester.D.	----- Ditto ----	---- ditto----	Nil.
1927.	Pte. McWatts. T.	----- Ditto ----	---- Ditto----	Nil.
3087.	Pte. Drain. T.	----- Ditto ----	---- Ditto----	Nil.
1626.	Pte. Buchanan.P.	WOUNDED IN ACTION 20/6/15.	O.C.Unit.	Not by O.C. Unit.
2578.	Pte. Lamont J.	-----Ditto------	---- Ditto---	--- Do---
2191.	Pte. Marr. C.	---- Ditto -----	---- Ditto---	--do-----
2206. WWPY.	Pte. Maxwell R.	Admitted 12 Field Ambulance 24/5/15.	O.C.12 Field Ambulance.	Nil.
1693.	Pte. Simpson.R.	WOUNDED IN ACTION 21/6/15.	O.C.Unit.	Not by O.C Unit.
1218.	Pte. Rankine T.	TRANSFERRED TO ENGLAND 13/5/15.	A.M.L.O. 24/5/15.	W'dd.
1413.	Dmr. Matheson.J.	TRANSFERRED TO ENGLAND 15/6/15.	O.C. H/S Oxfordshire	W"dd.
1992.	Pte. McLauhlan C.	TRANSFERRED TO ENGLAND 15/6/15.	---Ditto--	W'dd.

27/6/15.

CASUALTIES   No.1.DISTRICT

1/9th.Bn. ARGYLL & SUTHERLAND HIGHLANDERS.

Regtl. No.	Rank and Name	Casualty	By whom reported.	Prevs. reptd.
2665.	Pte. Taylor R.	WOUNDED & MISSING 10/5/15.	D.A.A.G2. Telegram dated 26/6/15.	"Wounded" only.

28/6/15.

J.A.Wood. Cpl.

CASUALTIES.   No.1 District.

1/9th Bn. Argyll & Sutherland Higherlanders.

Regtl. No.	Rank & Name	Casualty	By Whom Repd.	P.R.
1414	Pte. Brown J.	Transferred to England. 30/5/15.	O.C.Hosp. Ship St Andrew.	W.
1636	Pte. Hay A.	To Duty 20/6/15.	D.C.Bn. 26/6/15.	W.
1813	Pte. MELvin D.	do.	do.	S.
2620	Pte. McLean J.	do.	do.	W.
3169	Pte. Nugent R.	Do.	do.	W.
1529	Pte. Stevenson J.	do.	do.	W.
2486	Cpl. Bryden W.M.	do.	do.	W.
2507	Cpl. Cutland E.	do.	do.	W.
3032	Pte Cunningham D.	Do.	do.	W.
2609	Pte. McKinlay J.	do.	do.	W.
2655	Pte. Stevenson T.	do.	do.	W.
2025	Pte. Stoddart A.	do.	do.	W.
1691	Pte. Tosnie S.	do.	do.	W.
1496	Pte. Lindsay H.	do.	do.	W.
1385	Pte. Davidson J.	do.	do.	W.
2511	Pte. Clark J.	do.	do.	W.

30/6/15.

CASUALTIES   NO.1.DISTRICT.

1/9th.Bn. ARGYLL & SUTHERLAND HIGHLANDERS

Regtl. No.	Rank and Name	Casualty	By whom reptd.	Prevs. reptd.
2665.	Pte. Taylor. R.	Shrap. Wounds Legs.- Admitted 82nd Field Ambulance on 11/5/15 DIED on 11/5/15.	O.C. 82nd.Field Ambulance d/- 11/5/15.	"Wounded" & "Wounded and "Missing"

30/6/15.